AT THE LIMITS OF THE GAZE

AT THE LIMITS OF THE GAZE

SELECTED WRITINGS BY TAKUMA NAKAHIRA

Edited and translated by
Daniel Abbe and Franz Prichard

An Aperture Ideas Book

aperture

Contents

Editors' Note: Japanese names in this book appear in the Western style with the given name first, followed by the surname. Terms from Japanese are romanized using the modified Hepburn system. This includes, in particular, the use of macrons (ē, ō, ū) to represent the pronunciation of a long vowel.

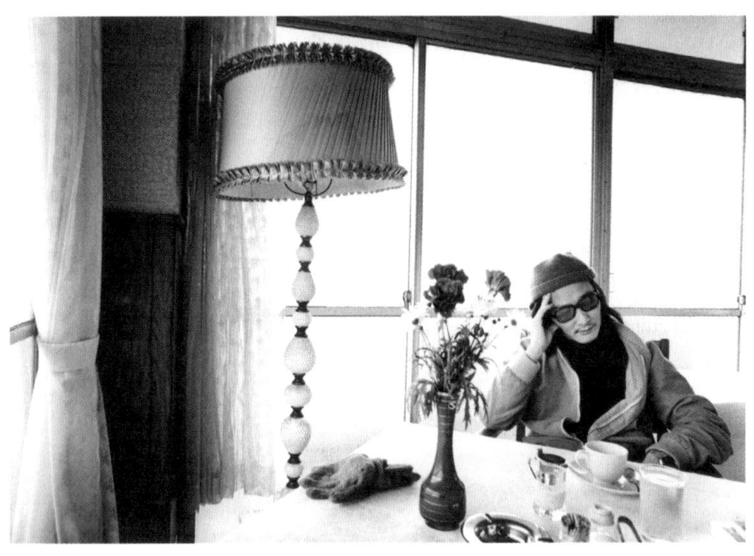

Takuma Nakahira in the coffee shop at the Nagisa Hotel in Zushi, Japan, February 1972. Photograph by Isao Sekiguchi

Foreword

Daniel Abbe and Franz Prichard

In 1962, Takuma Nakahira mailed a letter to Fidel Castro, expressing his desire to become a volunteer soldier for the Cuban Revolution. At the time, Nakahira was majoring in Spanish and participating in various leftist study groups about Latin America. In an article written about ten years later, Nakahira stated that the reply from Castro's secretary came back: "We are more than capable of defending our own country; you should fight in yours."

This early, perhaps apocryphal image of Nakahira nevertheless crystallizes a few key aspects of his work: a sustained interest in leftist politics, a field of view extending well beyond the borders of Japan, and also something of an impulsive streak. The writings that are collected in this volume—the first collection of Nakahira's essays to be published in English—might be called the result of the encounter between these expansive concerns and the specific medium of photography. That is why, even today, his written work invites us to consider photography not only as a creative medium but also as a means of questioning power.

After graduating college, Nakahira worked in Tokyo as an editor for the left-wing journal *Gendai no me* (Contemporary eye). This work put him in touch with major cultural figures of the day, including the poet and underground theater director Shūji Terayama and the photographer Shōmei Tōmatsu. Through Tōmatsu, Nakahira came to meet other prominent photographers like Yutaka Takanashi and Daidō Moriyama, as well as the critic and editor Kōji Taki. Soon enough, Nakahira quit his editor job and became a photographer. Along with poet and art critic Takahiko Okada, Nakahira, Taki, and Takanashi collectively founded the magazine *Provoke* in 1968, with Moriyama joining for two of its three issues. Setting out to reject established modes of photography, the members of *Provoke* published black-and-white images full of grain and contrast that pushed the bounds of visual legibility. While the novelty—and, in fact, the internal consistency—of the magazine's photography tends to be somewhat overstated, Nakahira is best known as a photographer for his *Provoke*-era work, which he collected in his 1970 photobook, *For a Language to Come*.

For all the attention paid to Nakahira's early photographs, his photography practice evolved together with his extensive work as an essayist, critic, and theorist. Nakahira raised questions about media and politics in print at a feverish pace, publishing more than one hundred essays between 1965 and 1977. The eleven essays here, written between 1970 and 1976, show Nakahira testing photography's capacity to help reimagine how we know and inhabit the world. They teem with the urgency of his historical moment, as the Cold War played out unevenly across the planet and irrevocably transformed the Japanese archipelago. Nakahira was part of a dynamic moment of artistic and political experimentation in Tokyo in which artists, filmmakers, sculptors, painters, theater directors, dancers, architects, and novelists were all engaged in discussing the relationship between art and power. While our selection introduces only one slice of Nakahira's career, the range of venues in which these essays were originally published—a literary review newspaper, an art magazine, a jazz magazine, and a photography magazine—shows just how far beyond the boundaries of photography Nakahira was thinking.

Born from this expansive moment of creative and critical encounters, Nakahira's writings developed through a ceaseless process of questioning, boring into the depths of specific concerns to pursue the contours of the world as an incomplete totality open to indeterminate possibilities. Throughout the nebula-like relations among Nakahira's writings, certain intertwined threads of questioning emerge. Each brings into view a different facet of entangled problems and potentials. Readers will surely find their own threads. To start, we might suggest the following three:

LANGUAGE AND IMAGE

Nakahira's writings interrogate the reduction of the world to representations of a human-centric outlook. To that end, he questioned photography's role as the mere illustration of existing language, or what he called the personal images of artists. Nakahira wagered that since language itself had become a code ordering the world, photography had the potential to break through this code and provoke, so to speak, new forms of relation. Although he originally aspired to be a poet, it was through photography that he set out to obtain a mode of language capable of bursting through the static and dualistic schema of self and world that is enshrined within the bourgeois subject. Like many thinkers of his era, Nakahira wrestled with the limitations of existing leftist political vocabularies and conservative humanist orthodoxies that became increasingly divorced from the actualities of the grinding destructive forces of corporate and state power. At stake in the evocative title *For a Language to Come* was not a self-enclosed system of photographic meaning, but rather an encounter with the silences of worlds that were emerging from the collapse of modernity's liberatory promises. Always pursuing the tension between image and language, Nakahira's own photography and writing trace the myriad forms of violence—and transformative possibilities to counter them—that give shape to the world that we now inhabit.

Nakahira connected photography to unconscious and sensorial aspects of human experience, often describing it in corporeal terms. For example, in "Why an Illustrated Botanical Guide?," he stated that "looking cannot happen apart from the body." He consistently wrote about the bodily effect that images—whether in printed media, on the wall, or broadcast on television—have before they reach the level of cognition. And yet, Nakahira's essays also demonstrate that he was an extremely cerebral writer who engaged with the intellectual currents of his time. Why, then, this concern with the body, not the head?

Several answers are possible, including Nakahira's abiding interest in Surrealism. As "The Will Toward History—Surrealism's Potential Power" shows, he was interested in reclaiming this movement's zeal for the "twinned liberations of sensation and society." And by thinking about the body in political ways, Nakahira was in fact very much of his moment. After all, the energies of liberation that emerged around 1968 in Japan were not funneled toward narrow or procedural political goals. In a more expansive mode, they held out the possibility of rethinking the very nature of experience. This was particularly true of women's liberation movements in Japan at this time, and although Nakahira did not seriously account for gender in his writing, he was interested in embodied forms of difference. Perhaps that is why, soon after writing that "looking cannot happen apart from the body," he claimed: "To look is also to expose the self to the gaze of the other." In this way, Nakahira hints that photography might prompt an embodied exchange, in which the photographer must relinquish some of the power that would otherwise accrue to them through the camera's one-sided gaze.

The urgency of Nakahira's writings speaks to the fact that he was considering photography's role across disparate landscapes of struggle. For Nakahira, diffuse networks of the nation-state and capital constituted an emergent "landscape" of power—a term that he theorized in parallel with the activist film theorist Masao Matsuda, and which appears in the essay "Rebellion Against the Landscape: Fire at the Limit of My Perpetual Gazing . . ." Here, Nakahira tried to think beyond urban space, which he called a "uniformly plastered-over 'landscape' sustained by power itself." As the essay "The Illusion Called Document" shows, he also considered the mass media itself as an environment of power, noting that a weeklong, nationwide television broadcast of a police siege on leftwing militants unconsciously reproduced bourgeois morality in its viewers. He brought these concerns to bear on the harsh realities of Okinawa, with which Japan had renewed colonial relations in 1972 following its reversion to mainland rule. Although Okinawa appears as the subject of only one essay included in this collection ("My Naked-Eye Reflex—1974, Okinawa, Summer"), Nakahira's later writings and photography address the possibility of working under and against Japan's extractive colonial relationship with the islands. He returns again and again to photography's role in both securing *and* unsettling capitalist modernity's varied landscapes of power, and to their environmental and human toll.

*

While aspects of these three overarching concerns can be found across the work collected here, it should be noted that Nakahira's essays are not the product of a comprehensive system of thought. Nakahira was not a full-time critic, much less an academic of any sort. He was a working photographer, and the essays in this volume were written freelance. Much like his photographs, then, Nakahira's essays could be thought of as performances in real time, in which he responded to the specific context of a particular journal, its audience, and the questions and sensations that struck him at that moment. While they may not add up to a complete whole, the reader can connect these different points, like stringing together the stars of a constellation.

This scattered quality sometimes extends to Nakahira's prose. His sentences have a tendency to twist around themselves, becoming extraordinarily long, while others are brusque and choppy, for bombastic effect. Although we have broken up most of these long sentences in our translation, we have also tried to preserve the rhythm and tone of his writing wherever possible. (While Nakahira never wrote a footnote in his life, for the sake of legibility we have converted his own inline citations to footnotes. Any additional notes were written by us.) In an era before word processors, Nakahira would have written these articles by hand, on a specialized kind of paper called *genkō yōshi*, a grid of small squares, each of which accommodates one character or punctuation mark; the sheets were then handed over directly to a magazine or newspaper editor. At times, one can imagine Nakahira filling up the *genkō yōshi*, thinking in real time, following his own stream of consciousness.

As traces of a lifelong practice of questioning, Nakahira's writing emerged through a transformative confrontation with a changing world. After a fever-induced coma in the fall of 1977, Nakahira experienced memory loss and partial aphasia that brought an end to his writing career. From that point on, he continued to raise new questions through his practice of photography, which he pursued for the rest of his life. In his later years, Nakahira once remarked that he smoked the "Short Hope" brand of cigarettes, noting: "There is also 'Long Hope,' but now is not an age that seeks world revolution."

The questions that Nakahira prompts may resonate even more acutely today, within the cascading violence and catastrophe of this world still at war with itself. While the moment of correspondence with Castro may belong to the past, perhaps contemporary readers can find forms of "short hope" in Nakahira's essays, which both suggest doubt about, and possibilities for, a photographically mediated reckoning with the world. At the limits of the possessive gaze perturbed by his ceaseless questioning, Nakahira shows us other ways of seeing and sharing the world with photography.

Kyoto and Tallahassee, January 2025

Daniel Abbe holds a PhD from the Department of Art History at the University of California, Los Angeles (UCLA), and is a lecturer at Osaka University of Arts.

Franz Prichard is an associate professor at Florida State University, author of *Residual Futures: The Urban Ecologies of Literary and Visual Media of 1960s and 1970s Japan* (2019), and has taught at UCLA, Harvard University, University of North Carolina at Charlotte, and Princeton University.

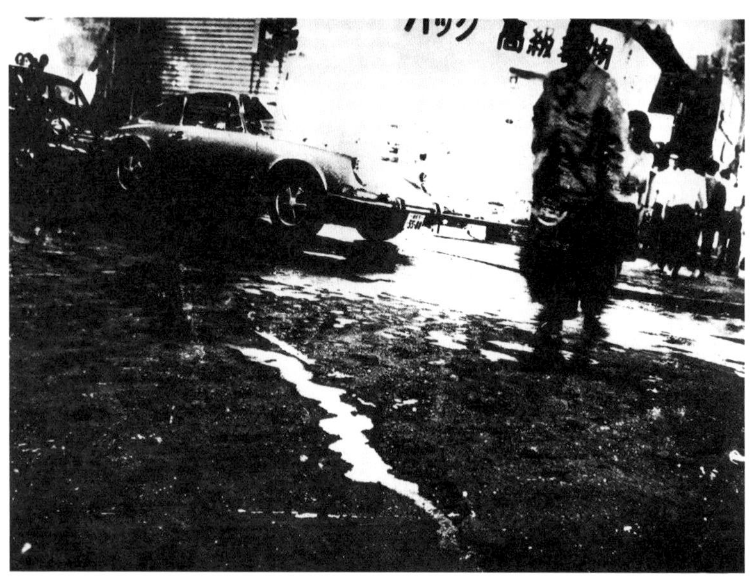

Takuma Nakahira, *Untitled*, from the photobook *For a Language to Come*, 1970

Has Photography Been Able to Provoke Language?

I once wrote about image [*eizō*] and language: "At one time it was declared that, opposing language, images had an independent meaning in themselves, and a 'language of images' was spoken about as though it were real. Yet this is surely mistaken. On the contrary, images haunt language like a shadow, they underpin language and give it substance, and in some cases, they amplify it."[1]

Although this may be a pretentious way of speaking, my thinking basically remains unchanged, even today. In fact, at the time I wrote that essay, I had just published the collectively produced magazine *Provoke*, which my four associates and I presumptuously subtitled "Provocative Materials for Thought."[2] I was concerned that the term *thought* had an overly political or philosophical resonance, and argued that, strictly speaking, it should be rephrased as "language as thought."

Two years on, have the photographs presented in *Provoke* been able to revive language in the end? Regrettably, my answer to this question would have to be somewhat negative. Strictly speaking, though, just what were the "language" and "image" that I claimed, in my garbled way, should be revived? This question now returns to confront me once again.

Just what are the hordes of words packed together into dictionaries like sardines? While they certainly constitute a language of the most basic universal signs that has been selected and approved by history, we cannot of course immediately accept them as lived language. I don't know when it started, but a strange delusion has taken up residence in some corner of my brain that I cannot shake free. Whenever I open the dictionary, the characters are rigidly organized, with a straight posture; for this very reason, they do not produce any deep feeling. But then, I imagine that once the dictionary is left closed up on my desk, each letter and each word argues for its validity, one by one, and a massive brawl ensues. At that moment, the words secretly spring to life, and regain their innate impact as language. But once I reach for the dictionary, the words sense this, and swiftly revert to their ordered state, in other words their dead, "constricted" state. Of course, this is clearly a childish, demented fantasy.

That is because, to the extent that language is not lived out by people, it consists of mere signs that vaguely indicate that a tree is a tree; language only comes to life when it is lived out by people, at which point the words in the dictionary break free of mere relational concepts, and transform themselves into what Roland Barthes calls "bursting words," "a vertically rising up language."[3]

Barthes writes: "The bursting upon us of the poetic word then institutes an absolute object; Nature becomes a succession of verticalities, of objects, suddenly standing erect, and filled with all their possibilities."[4] Although he is more directly describing the character of language in contemporary poetry, this also shows just what lived language is within the history that is the present day.

No matter how ingeniously it may have been assembled and developed, universal language, which is embedded within the notion of relations from the outset, is unable to grasp the world today. Such language is rooted in the arrogant modern rationalism that assumes it can entangle itself with the world in an organic relation.

On the contrary, lived language is absolutely not universal language, or language that presupposes relation. Instead, it discards the relation with totality, and exists as words "full of terror" that stand tall in the here and now.[5] By simply existing, or by simply being uttered, this language is like an isolated "object" full of wild energy, which can shake people to their core. It cannot be a serial, opened-up language that presupposes communication with others. Further, this "bursting language" is a language that is fiercely lived out in the here and now by a single person.

An image is always about something. It is an image, fixed on film, of a thing that exists here and now. It is not reality itself, but it always emerges from a certain relation of correspondence with reality. Thus, no matter how much an image may "not look like that," it must maintain, however narrowly, a relation with "that."

However, this is absolutely not to make the point that an image is proof of the self-evident but pointless logic that a tree is a tree. On the contrary, when we say "tree" and do not try to see a particular tree in reality but only try to see a generalized tree as meaning—if we then carefully observe a single tree before us here and "now," the word *tree* that we held, together with its concept and meaning, slowly breaks down. The image I am describing is one that, through this process, amplifies the substance of the word *tree* for each person who looks at it.

Through a certain optical relation, the camera surely fixes a single tree as a single tree on film. To that extent, the image is often confused with reality. Photographs like those used as proof of identity are one such example. But here, questions of the when, the where, and the who of looking are conveniently forgotten. This is true not only of identification photographs, but also of various kinds of photojournalism and documentary filmmaking that assert one realism or another. But in the end, does a universal tree, an objective tree, exist?

It may certainly exist, but to the extent that I am not present there, a tree has no meaning, and in the end, this tree would have no connection to people. A tree first comes about as a tree through the person who sees it. In the same way, a real thing is what appears as a real thing to me, here and now.

Godard has defined the films he makes as "wagered reality," which accurately describes these relations. Not reality itself, but a secondary reality that has been transformed and made subjective through my presence. That is an image.

To repeat, it is not possible for a photographer photographing a single tree to live with no connection to the word *tree*. As the word *tree* sticks to the photographer like a compulsive thought while he gazes at a single tree in reality inside the finder, that word suddenly crumbles, and he is present for the reformation of the tree as a new tree (which is "reality" in the true sense of the word).

So, what about someone looking at an image of a single tree? Of course, he cannot demand the experience of the photographer. That is because such persuasiveness (this is a word that is, precisely, rooted in seriality) cannot be asked of a single photograph. Just as a single photograph of a tree internally amplifies the language of the photographer who quoted the tree from reality, it also opens itself up to being re-quoted by each individual person that looks at it. In the end, whether the language of each person looking at a single photograph is amplified or not depends on the depth of their own engagement with language. Certainly, the levels of image and language are closely connected.

It seems that *Provoke* has fulfilled one of its roles, to overturn the image as proof of the self-evident but pointless logic that a tree is a tree. Against this, even if belatedly, it has presented images that raise doubts about meanings of resemblance taken for granted. Yet even this has now fallen into a kind of minor fashion, by which I do not refer simply to something customary, but instead to the very flesh and thought of each one of us that it comforts. Extremely grainy images, or intentionally unfocused photographs: these have already become mere decorations.

Today, we must return to the starting point. I cannot speak clearly about what form this will ultimately take. Having made clear that a tree is a tree, though, this must perhaps be something that widens the amplitude of the word *tree*, brought about through my presence with it in the here and now.

But how far this can go must be tested once again.

First published in the literary review newspaper *Nihon Dokusho Shimbun*, March 30, 1970. Later collected in *For a Language to Come* (Fūdosha, 1970) and *Why an Illustrated Botanical Guide? Collected Writings on Images by Takuma Nakahira* (Shōbunsha, 1973).

Notes

1 Here, Nakahira cites his essay "Can Photography Revive Language," published in the September 30, 1968, issue of *Nihon Dokusho Shimbun*. Throughout this essay, the word that Nakahira uses for image, *eizō*, refers specifically to an image that is produced through technical means, meaning that it could refer not just to photographs but also to cinema or television.

2 *Provoke* was a Tokyo-based magazine of photographs, essays, and poetry published across three issues, between 1968 and 1969. The members of the collective at its inception were Nakahira, Kōji Taki, Takahiko Okada, and Yutaka Takanashi. Daidō Moriyama joined from the second issue.

3 Here, Nakahira is likely paraphrasing Barthes in *Writing Degree Zero*, trans. Annette Lavers and Colin Smith (New York: Hill and Wang, 1968).

4 Ibid., 50.

5 Ibid.

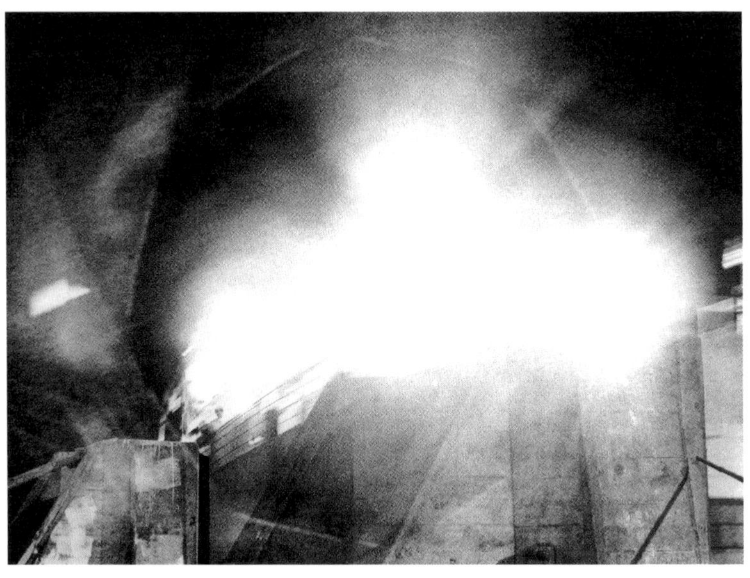

Takuma Nakahira, *Untitled*, from the photobook *For a Language to Come*, 1970

Rebellion Against the Landscape: Fire at the Limit of My Perpetual Gazing . . .

Although I have been given the topic of urban rebellion theory, to write about this as a purely strategic or tactical problem obviously exceeds the limits of my ability, and is probably not what has been asked of me. If that were the case, there are more accomplished experts out there.

And yet when combined in this way, the word *urban* and the word *rebellion* have a strangely alluring resonance that fills my heart with excitement. Urban, rebellion. Inside of me, for some reason, these words must appear at night, where a fire burns bright red, as if to make the night exist all the more as night. Of course, they must also be filled with terror and disquiet. Described in this way, my image of urban rebellion is very common, something that can all too easily be related to any single uprising, like the scenes of Shinjuku on October 21, 1968, between 10 p.m. and midnight, or of the East Gate of Kamata Station on the evening of November 16, 1969.[1] Even so, why a fire? And why at night?

The outstanding film critic Masao Matsuda once wrote that the "serial killer" Norio Nagayama wandered about from place to place in order to slash apart the uniformly plastered-over "landscape" sustained by power itself that appeared before his eyes, and that it was only for that purpose that he discovered the sound of a single gunshot within himself.[2] For me, too, the world only opens up before me as a solid "landscape," lustrous like plastic. While this is without question a travesty for my flesh and my senses, I could also say that it is for this very reason that I continue to take photographs. To be sure, the city cannot exist unconnected from this "landscape." No, instead, if anything the city is "landscape" itself. The violence and disorder of the city, and particularly of Tokyo, has frequently been pointed out. But this is nothing more than a *frame-up* by journalism and the social sciences. Even if murders and traffic accidents occur in the city every night, and industrial complexes spew forth poisonous gasses that shorten the lives of thousands of citizens, these are nothing more than natural selection, a preestablished harmony. Beyond a bit of chaos, a bit of poison, the real city still continues to exist today as a transparent "landscape" without a single scratch. Each night, the city wipes clean all impurities, acquiring a nearly perfect beauty. Then, it becomes an impregnable fortress, without so much as a single weakness. Precisely because of this, I must set this hostile "landscape" aflame with my own hands. A fire all of my own. Fire is the final form of sentiment. From that point, it is a question of meticulous tactics. (But that is revolution, not rebellion.)

One day, a single crack will cut into this uniformly plastered-over "landscape," and gradually deepen into a fissure, turning the "landscape" inside out like a glove being taken off the hand. Without question, this is rebellion. At that time, the "landscape" will no longer be a "landscape"; instead, it will become a crucible of confusion, trampled underfoot by the bare feet of flesh-and-blood people. Fire will engulf the entire city, in which people will run amok. Fire and darkness. People recklessly running around barefoot. In ancient times, people must have run around barefoot in the midst of fire and darkness. It may be an antiquated image, but the urban rebellion I secretly envision must resemble this.

The great waves of student power that swelled up the year before last offered some signs of urban rebellion, however slight. Since the end of last year, though, they appear to have quickly settled down. However, nothing will come of lamenting this fact. The question now is to ask what this one crack was, and how it can be made into a larger fissure. For example, just what was the "liberated district" of the Kanda Latin Quarter, which was temporarily realized on January 19, 1969?[3] Was the liberated district literally liberated? Was it a base of operations that should continue to be expanded? In other words, was it a space that achieved freedom on its own?

The "wrapping maniac" Christo is expected to come from New York to join the Mainichi International Art Exhibition that began on May 10 (I say "expected" because as I write this manuscript on May 1, I have not yet heard the news that he will come to Japan).[4] He got his start by making a barricade of oil barrels on a city street corner, calling it his own artwork. Then he began his urban wrapping works by using aerial photos of the city (New York, in this case) to make montages. He gradually became engrossed in the dream of wrapping things, and as he became dissatisfied with montage photographs, he turned to buildings in actual cities, wrapping them up with vinyl and tying them up with rope. Although he began wrapping up certain museums, and has most recently wrapped up kilometers of coastline in Australia, without a doubt his intention was to privately own public and historic cities by wrapping them up. The important thing is that this ownership was made possible by blockading and paralyzing the functions of the city. He didn't make anything in the usual sense, but I think he did more than "make something" by obstructing and blockading that order (which is, itself, landscape).

Christo's wrapping series immediately makes me think of the students' barricade blockade. The students realize their "objection" by first blockading the buildings of the universities where they stand. By blockading the public university—as a system, and as the very "landscape" that encompasses them—they attempt to own it individually. The logic that supports this strategy is surely the same as Christo's. In this case, the difference between Christo's wrapping for the sake of his conceptual works of art and the students' blockading as direct protests against power is not really much of a difference at all. After all, in the end, a work of art is nothing more than the trace of an artist's life, which is, strictly speaking, a life lived intensely by someone, and the students carried out their blockades as an inevitable gesture of their own "objection." Whether it was the city or the university campus, they took their surrounding environments, and the world, as a hostile "landscape," and then wrapped it up or blockaded it in order to slash it apart and blow it up. The actual substance of urban rebellion is the concrete form of the desperate struggles of separate individuals to personally possess for themselves the public, historic city (which is supported by nothing less than power itself). To return to the liberated district, it was definitely not a free space that achieved liberation on its own. As proof of this, the students' liberated district was temporary and localized, because from the beginning it emerged in a tense relation with the external "landscape" that enveloped it. It was nothing more than a single little crack in the absolutely dominant "landscape." Yet through that crack, the structure of the world has been manifested more clearly for the first time. Wrapped up by Christo, the coastline has been manifested for the first time as the coastline, and the city has been manifested for the first time as the city. In the same way, the students exposed the true form of the university by blockading their campuses.

Near the end of Michelangelo Antonioni's film *Zabriskie Point*, a young woman whose lover has been killed by the police escapes from a city (actually, it is a single building) among the towering cliffs of Death Valley. As she looks back on this magnificent city, her hostile gaze blows it up. Yet can a hateful glance blow up a city, or slash apart a "landscape"? As a professional photographer, this is an extremely pointed question for me.

Even now, the world is before me as an expressionless, uniform "landscape." And as it becomes more beautiful, its coherence will probably become more perfect. To tell the truth, I am like a scrawny dog sniffing about for a vulnerable crevice that may not even exist; what I seek is the remote possibility of a single crack in this perfect "landscape." Is there no hidden crevice that would offer a sign of even a single crack within this smoothed-over, beautiful "landscape"? If I could only find such a crevice, wouldn't the city, and "landscape," crumble away under my angry gaze just like the city blown to pieces in *Zabriskie Point*? But this is just a crazy delusion. There is no crevice, or anything like it. Perhaps it can only be discovered through fire, rocks, or rifles.

For the time being, there is no other method for me than to continuously gaze at this "landscape." Yet, at the limits of my perpetual gazing, could a fire, my real fire, be igniting? I won't know without trying. But I can say for sure that this is only possible by completely transforming myself into my fire. After all, seeing is unrelated to *doing*. This is true even if *doing* first becomes clear through seeing.

Urban rebellion. An unrestrained personal invasion against "landscape." It is the concretization of a dream endlessly repeated by many people to somehow change the political order (even if it is unlikely to change).

First published in the art magazine *Graphication*, June 1970. Later collected in *For a Language to Come* (Fūdosha, 1970).

Notes

1 The Shinjuku riots of 1968 erupted when protestors, in honor of International Anti-War Day, besieged Shinjuku Station to protest the refueling of US war planes in Japan. Another violent clash erupted at Kamata Station in 1969, near Tokyo's Haneda Airport, where protestors attempted to disrupt Prime Minister Eisaku Satō's visit to the US.

2 Along with Nakahira, Masao Matsuda (1933–2020) was a key figure in the discourse around "landscape theory," or *fūkeiron* in Japanese, which articulated a relationship between state power and landscape through images. Matsuda was involved in making the 1969 film *A.K.A. Serial Killer*, which took Norio Nagayama as its subject.

3 The Kanda Latin Quarter was a student barricade inspired by the events of May 1968 in Paris. A group of student activists blocked off a major street in central Tokyo during violent police assaults on Tokyo University, where students had occupied a building.

4 The exhibition Nakahira is referring to is commonly known as *Tokyo Biennale '70: Between Man and Matter*. Curated by Yūsuke Nakahara, it brought together a group of forty artists from Japan and overseas, many of whom were developing practices of conceptual art. In addition to Christo, some of the well-known participating artists included Hans Haacke, On Kawara, Jannis Kounellis, Richard Serra, and Jirō Takamatsu. A photograph taken by Nakahira appeared on the cover of the Biennale catalog, and the official poster of the exhibition featured another of his photographs.

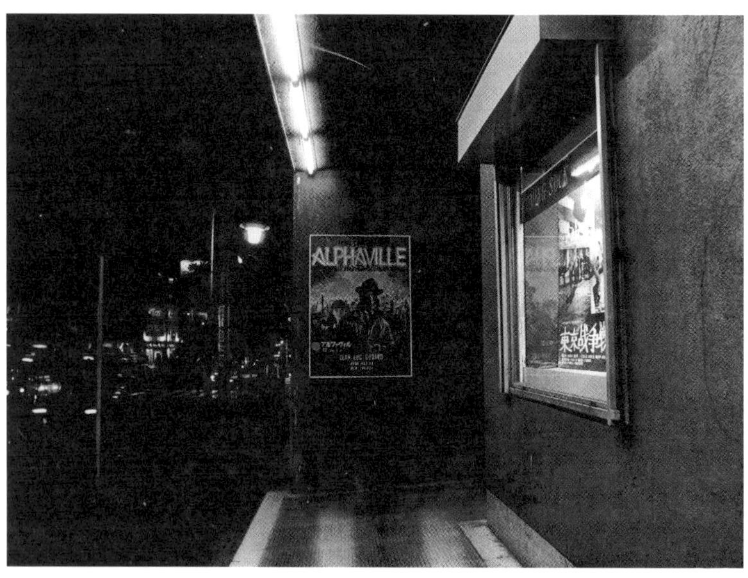

Takuma Nakahira, *Untitled*, from the photobook *For a Language to Come*, 1970

The Work of Art Is a Part of Reality

It has already been about a month since I watched Godard's *Wind from the East*.[1] Yet, I still can't decide whether this film is "good" or "bad." Especially because a significant amount of entertainment value is expected of films, filmgoers judge them too easily according to just two words: whether it was "good" or "bad."

What is described as film analysis and film critique, imbued with the pretentious knowledge and individualistic tastes fancied by intellectuals, is in the end just an explanation of these two adjectives, "good" or "bad" (grammatically, I am not sure if they are adjectives).

But if it is possible to loosely categorize Godard's works just before *La Chinoise*—namely from *My Life to Live* to *Weekend*—in terms of "good" or "bad," both *La Chinoise* and its excessive remake *Wind from the East* completely deviate from this adjectival system of evaluation. They go beyond it, and become something entirely different. People try to personally own films, literature, and "works of art" of all kinds by attaching adjectives such as beautiful, sad, hopeful, or pessimistic to them.

By doing so, these receivers preserve a preestablished and harmonious distance between themselves and the "work of art." When an even more suitable adjective is found, this distance becomes all the more stable. There is the world, there is the self, there is the "work of art" and the self who receives it. However, Godard has blurred these very relations.

Actually, no—he has torn them apart. Makoto Satō's extremely affective comment on this film—"Ah! He did it, he did it"—seems to be related to this.[2] To return to the issue of adjectives, it is no longer possible to attach any to *Wind from the East*. *Wind from the East* stands tall, refusing all of them. If forced, one could very tentatively throw out an adjective like "awesome," an adjective that is not really one, and which does not help to understand what is "awesome" here—and then one would forget the film.

Accumulations of juxtaposed shots, nearly static frames, huge numbers of quotations from books and their recitation are all extremely distinctive features of Godard's previous films. In particular, *La Chinoise* could be considered a prototype of *Wind from the East.* However, the cool indifference akin to an intellectual game that still remains in *La Chinoise* is completely wiped away here.

In *La Chinoise*, for example, after a man who is expelled by the Maoist student group returns to the French Communist Party, there is a scene of him eating bread in the middle of a heated debate; there is no such comedy here. A Communist Party represented wolfing down bread—in Japan, this would look like a Communist Party member who eats a pork cutlet and rice bowl during a debate, and we would certainly laugh at it. There is, at least, some metaphor or allegory of "reality" there.

To be precise, *Wind from the East* is not something that can be called a "work of art" in the usual sense. At least, it is not a "work of art" that follows the formula that there is "reality" and an "artist," and then the "work of art" that connects them. There, the world is a concluded cosmos, and the "work of art" is a microcosmos that, at the end of the day, symbolizes, points to, and re-concludes the world. The "artist," in turn, mediates this process. In *Wind from the East*, this happy relation is torn apart.

While only a few have called for "the abolition of art" or "the abolition of expression," it is because of art and expression's fundamentally conservative and reactionary quality that this call has been made (mainly, in the essay "The Abolition of Art" by art critic Alain Jouffroy).[3] But there are extremely few examples, even preliminary ones, where this has been carried over to practice. This is especially the case for films.

I felt a certain amount of resistance to calling the events of May 1968 in Paris—where only two or three people died—a revolution or something similar, although things like "Paris May Revolution" were said, whether because of the Latin Quarter, or because of the famous words "All Power to the Imagination" that were written on the walls there. Particularly in Japan, it was received in a way that made it fashionable. Through newspapers, TV, and so-called documents, we now know Paris May '68 as information so thoroughly as to be sick of it.

However, I have to confess that through watching Godard's "fabrication" in *Wind from the East*, I came to know for the first time that Paris '68 was in fact a tremendous turning point in history, and that it truly was a revolution, which ended in miscarriage.

In a long scene where Anne Wiazemsky is intermittently strangled by a man wearing a military uniform from the American Civil War, and where a huge amount of red ink "suggestive of blood" pours in from the outside, in other words from the side of the camera, I saw Paris '68. This liquid looks nothing like blood, and could only be red ink. Paradoxically, through Godard's very fabrication, which makes explicit that red ink is nothing but red ink, I saw Paris '68.

But I must make clear: this does not mean that *Wind from the East* has skillfully "expressed" Paris, or that it has accurately captured "reality." Instead, *Wind from the East* is already a part of "reality." I have not seen them, but the countless flyers that must have covered the walls of Paris '68 were not signs that simply represented revolution; they were truly revolution itself, and in the same way, *Wind from the East* is also a part of reality.

Truly, Godard sees the world. Yet, it is a paradox that to look at the world is also to be a part of the world. To call this, somewhat pompously, "the otherness of the self" doesn't help anything. Those who look carefully will inevitably discover the self that is being looked at.

We cannot ignore this split and become entranced by the slightly arty rhetoric of image, imagination, fantasy, and the like. This, at least, is our age.

First published in the literary review newspaper *Nihon Dokusho Shimbun*, August 17, 1970. Later collected in *For a Language to Come* (Fūdosha, 1970) and *Why an Illustrated Botanical Guide? Collected Writings on Images by Takuma Nakahira* (Shōbunsha, 1973).

Notes

1 Jean-Luc Godard (1930–2022) was a French and Swiss film director, known as a key figure of French New Wave cinema. Strictly speaking, *Wind from the East* (1970) was collectively produced by the Dziga Vertov Group, a filmmaking cooperative in which Godard participated.

2 Makoto Satō (1943–) is a Japanese theater director; he is known as a leading figure of the *Angura* (or "underground") theater movement of the 1960s and 1970s.

3 Alain Jouffroy (1928–2015) was a French art critic who made the first call for an Art Strike in "The Abolition of Art," which has not been translated into English at the time of writing. Nakahira cites this essay in "Why an Illustrated Botanical Guide?," collected in this volume; see page 91.

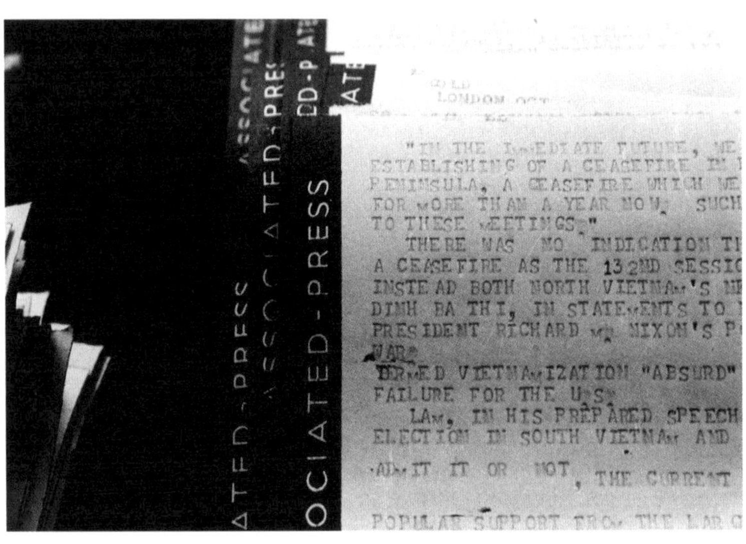

Takuma Nakahira, *Untitled*, from the series *Circulation: Date, Place, Events*, 1971

The Illusion Called Document: From Document to Monument

1

Photographs are documents. From the invention of photography to the present day, this has been long believed to be the primary material premise of photography. Certainly, the thesis that a photograph is a document is obvious beyond any doubt, at least when considering the optical mechanisms of film and camera. This becomes even more obvious when one considers that a technical image [*eizō*] is always an image of something, and that a technical image that springs forth independently of the outside world is a logical contradiction. What makes a photograph a photograph goes beyond the consciousness of the photographer, or whoever is operating the camera; the meaning of the thing that is represented only emerges from within the potential understanding between the person taking the photograph and the person who looks at it. At that time, no person can doubt that a photograph is a document.

But this physical character of a photograph has been tied to its social character in an unmediated way. From the time that this was uncritically accepted, not just photographs but television, films, and other kinds of technical images in general now reveal that this dangerous condition was already being prepared at some fundamental level.[1] In this era of the "information society," hasn't this been the decisive factor in separating reality from images, and in their subsequent emergence as fetishes, not just at a social level but, above all, inside our own consciousness?

To put things a little more concretely: yes, through the directness of reflecting reality, photography has succeeded at considerably reducing the distance between reality and ourselves. If photography has any great potentiality in comparison to other media, it lies here. In particular, when photography, which was developed essentially as a modern, reproducible technique, merged with the even more reproducible technique of printing, the latent potential of the camera was converted into an obvious power. Initially, this succeeded in forcibly bringing individuals close to realities that had been distant, at the very least for the large number of readers within the circulation of such publications. Later, this took a more pointed and widespread form, as films and television took on a spellbinding power from which something like escape is almost impossible. These images directly couple us to reality because they are truly its resemblance, and all of the simultaneously happening events in reality are practically force-fed to each of us.

Today, whether we like it or not, we are confronted with countless mass-produced realities—fragmentary ones at that—through the vast quantities of printed materials that are delivered to us (newspapers, magazines, flyers, catalogs) and the television that is broadcast almost throughout the entire day. In a sense, there has never been a time in which we were so thoroughly immersed in reality as we are today. That is the case in formal terms, at least. But whether that reality is actually something we lived out or not is an absolutely different question. Beyond this, we forget that a technical image cut out from reality is no more than an image of reality. Through a short circuit, we take it all too easily for reality itself; this may be why we believe that reality itself is not reality, but the image of reality. This is the first thing we must investigate.

Clearly, we are living inside a strange myth. This is the immanent logic that supports the information society, from our side, the logic of the optical illusion that reality is not reality but instead the image of reality. Or perhaps it is deeply connected to the historical formation of our senses, which simply confuse the reality that is captured in a technical image with reality when the physical condition that a photograph is a document of reality expands to the social level. Needless to say, within the present capitalist system, this is something that power imposes upon and demands of us. This is the mediating "consciousness industry," in which all information is controlled and sold to us as commodities. The important point here is that technical images themselves are also already controlled and manipulated. In the case of other media, such as print media, within the information that they present to us it is easier to sniff out the industrial language, and finally the political form that supports industrial society—that is to say, the language of the state. Perhaps we have acquired enough knowledge to make it relatively easy to spot this because of print media's long history. However, our mechanical belief in the documentary quality of technical images is so deeply rooted in us that it is difficult to rip out; when it comes to these images or to photographs, we are all too easily disarmed. But it's the same in both cases. Despite the *myth of universality* spread by the bourgeoisie, in capitalist society we are inevitably divided into exploiter and exploited. There can be no reconciliation between these two sides. The essence of this situation should appear even more clearly in the image media of today's information society. However, since we believe in the primary documentary quality of technical images—that everything reflected there is really happening—our senses constitute another side of the situation. Our senses obscure the bourgeoisie's skilled tricks, and allow us to accept the idea that the only reality is the reality that has been made into a technical image. The power to select is entirely in the grasp of industry, capital, and the state. Having lost access to a circuit of reciprocal communication, the masses are placed in the one-sided position of a consumer of information.

At most, a single photograph taken by a single photographer is also the result of a selection. The reality reproduced there bears no resemblance to the reality that expands just a centimeter beyond the frame. It is often pointed out that photography is not about making, but selecting. That is indeed the case. It is impossible for a technical image to come into existence from nothing. But what happens if, from this basic point, we then believe that the only reality is the reality that is selected by massively powerful organizations and then assigned to us? We would unconditionally hand over all of our freedom to the other side.

Before, I wrote that the bourgeoisie arises from class-based profit, which it thoroughly protects using the form of the nation, puffing up the illusion that they and the people they exploit are all equal citizens united in the state. In this way, they universalize the morality of the ruling class as the morality of all people, and thus extend their exploitation even to our own consciousness. It seems to me that there is a strange parallel between this and our present problem of the information industry's swindles that push us to believe that all of the realities that are reproduced in technical images actually happened. Or maybe the crystallized expression of this problem appears in the mass media, beginning with television. Bourgeois morals are sublimated as the general morals of humanity, and the reality of technical images is replaced by a universal reality. In any case, if nothing else, it is certain that here the masses, the people, are being skillfully manipulated through the ruling classes' guise of universality.

In Hans Magnus Enzensberger's excellent theory of mass media, "Constituents of a Theory of the Media," he sharply and concretely analyzes the manipulation of the people's consciousness through mass media, in particular televised images.[2] Enzensberger defines *manipulation* in the following way:

> The process of reproduction reacts on the object reproduced and alters it fundamentally. The effects of this have not yet been adequately explained epistemologically. The categorical uncertainties over whether something is real or fake also destabilize the concept of the documentary. Strictly speaking, it has shrunk to its legal dimensions.

> A document is something the "forging," i.e., the reproduction of which, is punishable by imprisonment. . . . The productions of the electronic media, by their nature, evade such distinctions as those between documentary and feature films. They are in every case explicitly determined by the given situation. The producer can never pretend, like the traditional novelist, "to stand above things." He is therefore partisan from the start. This fact finds formal expression in his techniques. Cutting, editing, dubbing—these are techniques for conscious manipulation without which the use of the new media is inconceivable. It is precisely in these work processes that their productive power reveals itself—and here there is no distinction to be made between a production of a reportage or a production of comedy. The material, whether "documentary" or "fiction," is in each case only a prototype, a half-finished article, and the more closely one examines its origins, the more blurred the difference becomes. (To elaborate further, *the reality in which a camera turns up is always a "staged" reality, e.g., the moon landing.*)[3]

This is a somewhat long quotation, but it says everything. Enzensberger speaks of the fusion of "documentary" with "fiction," through which, at the same time that all documents of reality are documents of reality, they also all become fictionalized once they pass through the media's manipulation and the cathode-ray tube of the television. Clearly, this is the case. While individual documents of reality remain documents of reality as fragments, they have no orientation at all. They only acquire a clear orientation and persuasiveness through their combination, or even before that, through the criteria that determine which fragments will be selected.

Let me cite a recent example. In March 1972, the holing up of the United Red Army group in the Asama Lodge was continuously broadcast on television for more than one week.[4] The final "battle" of the "siege of Asama Lodge" was broadcast for an entire day. Viewership rates reached unprecedented levels, but leaving that aside, I am extremely interested in this full week of television broadcasting, right down to the last day, along with the pictures that were broadcast. As is well known, during the week or so that the United Red Army was holed up inside Asama Lodge, it was impossible to see anything happening in the lodge from the outside. Adding the commentary that the students had been holed up for twenty-four hours, two days, three days, each television station continued to broadcast almost the same picture from the same position, looking up at the facade of a lodge in snowy Karuizawa. Each channel's long shot was taken from a fixed position; they all had more or less the same angle. Nothing about these records was "dramatic." Even so, every hour, on the hour, these stations obstinately broadcast a "newsflash" with the same shot. They could only transmit the information that several armed "criminals" had taken hostages and were, still, holed up inside. But with the passage of time, people realized that this televised image of the lodge's facade began to change a little within their minds. Such obstinate repetition began to enforce a morality. In other words, for the viewers in their living rooms, the "ferocity of the criminals" slowly became more distinct from the first day to the second, and from the second day to the third. The people in the lodge became "evil" as the days went on. Then, just as the moral balance of right-minded citizens had crossed the horizon that "it is natural to shoot criminals dead," the final siege was carried out. The police forces certainly calculated the timing of this action extremely carefully. And in the end, each television channel collaborated with the police by broadcasting images of the siege. Whether this collaboration was conscious or unconscious is almost entirely irrelevant. The point is that the police developed their "Do-or-Die Hostage Rescue Operation" on the assumed basis of the workings of the mass media—television first and foremost, but newspapers, magazines, and other outlets as well. For their part, the mass media clearly profited from the event: newspapers and magazines expanded their readership, while television channels secured high ratings.

So, what exactly was this fixed image of the lodge's facade, which was broadcast for a week? Much more so than a document, I think it was very strongly wrapped up with the qualities of a monument. The individual images conveyed nothing of the activity at the lodge. Because they could not convey what was actually happening inside, they could not be documents of reality, nor even documents good enough to give the sense of reality laid bare in technical images. Rather than a document, they were bathed in the colors of meaning. The individual images took on an extremely symbolic character. They were transformed into symbols signifying a "heinous incident" perpetrated by "heinous criminals." Here, though, the usual meaning of "symbol" does not quite fit. Instead, through the *live broadcast of a fixed view*, they were sublimated into something truly monumental.

The following facts can be drawn from this situation. First is the astounding fact that technical images manipulate and control the orientation of our consciousness. This manipulation starts by determining the orientation of our unconscious and ends with each of our own individual consciousnesses, even of our morals. Second is the fact that technical images are not formed simply by the meanings of reality that they copy, but that they themselves break free from this and transform into monumental fetishes of meaning. "Staged reality" goes well beyond its usual bounds and is made up into a new reality, with a meaning it determines itself. The crucial point is that what first makes this possible is the shared illusion of tacit deceit between sender and receiver that these images are fundamentally documents of things actually happening.

Although I took up the example of the television broadcast of Asama Lodge, the situation was clearly the same in the photographs and headlines of newspapers and magazines covering this incident. Readers will certainly remember having seen the same wide-angle photograph day after day, together with a barely modified headline. For more than a week, the pictures did not show anything new at all. And yet, we continued to gaze intently at those unchanging images of the lodge. What does this fact mean? Of course, we cannot deny the fact that we watched with bated breath, as though glued to our televisions, anticipating the conclusion of this drama that had to come sooner or later. But these images did not in any way fulfill the function that we have come to believe of them, in other words to replace something that we cannot see with something that we can. On the contrary, in this moment the indicative or exhibition function of technical images has been lost, and replaced with a symbolic function. What kind of symbol? The meaning of the incident cannot be properly grasped, because it is still unfolding in real time.[5] Even so, television, newspapers, and the mass media as a whole have already settled its meaning, i.e., the disclosure of the socially harmful and degenerate nature of a small number of extremists, as the consequence of the generalized rebellion that erupted at the end of the 1960s. The state, the police, and the mass media expected that the situation would inevitably reach a conclusion in accordance with this meaning. Working backwards from here, we can see how technical images were trotted out. In other words, the power of these individual televised images to evoke reality could only operate at a secondary order of meaning. This was, in sum, an inversion of the process that would effectively expose the totalized flow and meaning of the incident. The only role that news flashes, and the static images of the lodge attached to them, carried out was to drag viewers and readers along toward this conclusion. I think we can say this was thoroughly accomplished. The yearnings of the masses for raw reality on the other side of the cathode-ray tube certainly supported such an outcome. No longer transparent screens pointing to reality, images were transformed into the symbols and monuments of meanings to come. The absolutely mundane wide-angle photographs of the lodge were transformed into monuments, by wrapping us viewers up in countless emotional attachments. Technical images are no longer windows that open onto reality but are becoming sacred icons unto themselves.

Walter Benjamin wrote that the invention of photography transformed the cult value that art had held up until that point. The indicative function of photography changed this cult value into exhibition value. This is already an extremely famous discourse, but just thirty years after it was written, the situation has again turned on its head, as exhibition value looks to have taken on a new cult value.[6] Of course, what determines the value of each individual photograph is still what is in the photograph—that is, its indicative or exhibition function. Photographs are essentially like this, but when they take on the form that manifests in society, especially today's information society, I think that they again take on a cult value. As Enzensberger points out, this is deeply related to the existence of the consciousness industry, which manipulates each individual image, orders it within a single chain of meaning, and broadcasts it as reality. The consciousness industry tailors great amounts of information into profit-generating commodities and distributes them according to the ability of the masses to consume them. Who, after all, wants to buy a commodity without any cult value?

Obviously, what I have just narrated is an unavoidable condition for us photographers, who can work only within the mass media. To run away from this condition, by simply condemning it and raising a vain banner of "moral defeat," only leads to pridefulness in one's innocence. If that is the case, what should we do? This is the real question that confronts us today.

2

Let me turn to *Provoke*. Perhaps this will be nothing more than my private thoughts. Still, what were we trying to do? What did we accomplish, and what were we not able to? *Provoke* had no clear consciousness of being a movement. More than any prospect of a movement, I think what supported us was the extremely primitive impulse to do things that were not possible within the dominant photography and media of that time. For that reason, we did not necessarily share the same sense of what questions to pursue. This is the main reason why we had to end the publication after just three issues. So, I cannot sum up *Provoke*; at most, I can only offer a private self-criticism of my activities in and around *Provoke* at the time of my participation, from 1968 to 1970.

What supported us was the impulse to reject the photography that was dominant at that time, and is even more so today: a photography which clings to meaning, which begins and ends with meaning, and which understands photographs as illustrations of established language, reducible to meaning. Technical images cannot exist apart from language. In fact, all they can do is cling to language, and at times provoke or amplify it. It would have been better to replace the magazine's subtitle, "Provocative Documents for Thought," with "Provocative Documents for Language." This rough orientation was what we all shared. At the same time, I claimed that photographs were documents: "The fragments of reality cut out by the square frame are, for me, unbracketed realities that have emerged as intense realities that I myself lived. I myself cannot understand how I became inextricably involved with such fragments. And not just that—I still do not understand after one of my photographs is exhibited, printed, and distributed en masse. For me, who lived that moment, they are nothing more than the vivid real. In this way, one single photograph is incorporated into my personal history. When I pick up the camera again, the darkness of my whole life weighs upon the finger that is on the shutter."[7]

Thinking about it now, my claim that photographs are documents was an antithesis of the prevailing theories of this type, namely naturalist realism and socialist realism. The former relies on the physical characteristics of the camera and tries to limit photographs to their informational value of making faraway things near, or invisible things visible. Since the birth of photography, this tenuous theory has stubbornly clung to photographers. Socialist realism is almost exactly the other side of the coin. (Out of the sense of duty that it needs to indict the present age, it records only the dirty and ugly places of its time. In the sense that the thought and epistemology of socialist realism provides no space to doubt existing words and meaning, it is exactly the same as naturalist realism. The only difference between them is the corner in which they run and hide.)

Against these theories, I pit documents of the life I was living. Reality is not just the fact that a car is a car. Clearly, a car is a car, but this is an unproductive truth. I think that the only ground for my claims was that a car is composed of various individual realities, each carried by the person that sees or touches it within the totality of their own life. In other words, against our immediate association of the word *document* with an objective, impersonal viewpoint, I wanted to rethink this word through an emphasis only on the endless encounter between the world and the self. But in a certain sense, my attempt might have only rehashed the old and hoary theory of subjectivity. Of course, I understood that an image actually taken by a camera is a form of the world that exceeds any of the photographer's thoughts—it is itself a transcendental world, which always exists beyond the self. That is why I concluded that individual photographs were nothing more than traces of the life I lived: I myself am the structure of a perpetual and reciprocal movement in which the world constantly rejects me, and I exceed the world.

But could it really be so easy to declare that these photographs were nothing more than the traces of the life I lived? Actually, within the claim that each individual photograph is a trace of the life I lived lies the assumption that seeing is all there is to the experience of life, or at least that it is its main element. But it is obvious that our experience of life is something much more holistic, or rather bodily. It would be far more appropriate to say that for the photographer, one of their photographs is self-alienation given form. I visualize my lived experience in a single photograph, which is eventually published through mass media—like it or not, doesn't that unfairly and completely minimalize the life I lived? Most of the anonymous readers looked at my photographs just like they would a catalog photo, lacking the fullness of my life. But because I asserted that a photograph is a document, I certainly believed that some kind of communication, however uncertain, would emerge between the photograph and the readers. I think this is because I lacked the real consciousness that any kind of personal expression through photography is impossible outside of the social base on which photographs rely, in other words the mass media, the subject of this article.

By reducing all of my lived experience to seeing, and even further, by publishing this in the mass media, what emerged was something doubly alienated, with no trace of myself at all. The circuits to and from myself have been torn to shreds. But to what extent should a photographer take this on?

Now, if I look at things with a clear head, I can see that *Provoke* was trying to grab hold of an embodied speech (*parole*) for photographers. The idea was to use this embodied speech to cut through the existing visual language (*langue*) of aesthetics and values, which are ordered in a systematic way.[8] Of course, only a third party can judge how well the magazine was able to do that. But I have absolutely no optimistic observations, because it is certain that the embodied speech that *Provoke* was perhaps able to grasp was, in the next instant, swallowed up by the systematized mode of vision. On the contrary, if we discovered anything through *Provoke*, it was only the impregnable and multilayered structure of this age. As an example, certain technical aspects of photography—grain and blur that, to an even arrogant degree, we believed resulted from a direct encounter between the self and the world, or from raw lived experience—were swiftly transformed into design elements. As a result, our ostensibly rebellious stance and photography were liberally accepted as rebellious feelings and moods, completely watering down any rebellion that might have been there.

Back when the National Railway first rolled out its ridiculous and haughty tourism campaign, "Discover Japan," a friend joked to me: "Hey, *Provoke* is a big deal now, even the National Railway's gone blurry!" But it's no joke—on the contrary, it's ironic proof that they can take anything and water it down, only leaving behind its hollowed-out form. Or maybe this only captures half of the situation. From the instant that we are accepted, we ourselves start to rot. As a result, from that point on *are bure* changed into our "style."[9] This had already started around the time that people in the photography world were making a big fuss over the question of "Conpora or Realism."[10] I've digressed a bit here, but I simply wanted to discuss the questions *Provoke* raised and their limits. I am a photographer, so I can only speak from the position of a person taking photographs.

We tried to articulate a personal embodied speech through the method of photography, a method that did not simply emerge alongside mass media but developed as an essential part of it. This was a logical contradiction, but if anything might have made this articulation possible, it would certainly have been the fact that we chose to use the form of the collectively produced magazine, a polar opposite of the mass media. Through a small-run, collectively produced magazine of photography, we tried to return photography—fundamentally a technique of mass reproduction—to a personal relation between individuals. This was a valuable attempt for us, but it was fundamentally limited. Why? Because it was just a pipe dream to think that we could start from that miniature liberated zone and expand outward in concentric circles, overturning all relations as we went. Like all liberated zones, such as the one in Paris's Latin Quarter, *Provoke* demonstrated that when a free space is established temporarily, it only makes the completely unfree space surrounding it all the more manifest. That is all we were able to achieve.

Contemporary mass media is currently under the unilateral control of power. In order to convert all reality into informational value—in other words, into a commodity—it manipulates and manages reality. It presents only the reality that suits our tastes as reality. However, to reject the possibility of the mass media and retreat into a "logic of the handmade" resolves nothing. Enzensberger writes:

> At the very beginning of the student revolt, during the Free Speech Movement at Berkeley, the computer was a favorite target for aggression. Interest in the Third World is not always free from motives based on antagonism toward civilization which has its source in conservative culture critique. During the May events in Paris the reversion to archaic forms of production was particularly characteristic. Instead of carrying out agitation among the workers in a modern offset press, the students printed their posters on the hand presses of the École des Beaux-Arts. The political slogans were hand-painted; stencils would certainly have made it possible to produce them en masse, but it would have offended the creative imagination of the authors. The ability to make proper strategic use of the most advanced media was lacking. It was not the radio headquarters that were seized by the rebels, but the Odéon Theatre, steeped in tradition.[11]

Of course, in the manner of the Luddite movement, the impulse to smash the symbolic forces of production of an era at the beginning of a struggle is fully understandable. In this way, they could antagonize their era and obtain a kernel of autonomy. But of course, if things end there, that does not add up to the full meaning of a historical revolution.

On the contrary, the concrete and direct task that now faces us is to figure out how and where to start eating away at the mass media, which wields such authority today. I probably won't participate in another collectively produced magazine of photography. The feeling of self-satisfaction that emerges from it is no more than a drastic escape from today's reality. Once the photographs that I claimed are the documents of my own raw experience pass through the mass media, they are translated into a systematized vision, far removed from the directness of my life, in the blink of an eye. It is altogether too optimistic to deal with this by saying that a work turns into a completely different creature once it leaves my hand, or to adopt the attitude that everything can be left up to the contingency of some uncertain communication taking place. If I am to thoroughly commit to my life, I have to take responsibility for its final form. And there is no such thing as content without form.

The mass media have cleverly taken advantage of the naive understanding that a photograph is a document of reality, spreading the mass illusion that if it's in a photograph, it must be real. At the same time, the reverse is also true: anything not documented in a photograph or broadcast on television is thought to not be real. As a photographer, what am I to think about this situation? I would like to take up this question now.

3

A police officer died during the general strike and protest against the Okinawa Reversion Agreement that took place throughout Okinawa on November 10, 1971. On November 16, a young man from Saitama Prefecture was arrested as a murder suspect in the case, on the sole "evidence" of two photographs of the "site of the police officer's murder" taken by a freelance photographer that had been published in the morning edition of the November 11 issue of the *Yomiuri Shimbun*. From that point on until now, more than half a year later, the young man has been detained. The following caption was appended to the two photographs: "Sergeant Yamakawa (inside circle) showered with blows (above) and Molotov cocktails (below) by surrounding extremists." The face of the young man appears in the photographs, but according to the testimonies of people who were there at the time, he was in fact trying to rescue the sergeant who was engulfed in flames. Through these explanations, the very same two photographs take on completely opposite meanings. I do not know which one is correct. But speaking from my own experience, I think that no one joins a demonstration in order to kick an already-burning police officer to death. In any case, this will become clear from the trial.[12]

The important thing here is that at the same time that the *Yomiuri Shimbun* published these photographs and labeled them as the decisive moment of the crime, the prosecution fully believed everything about them and used them as its only "evidence" to make the arrest. While these are two different things, in the end they are intertwined by common interests. On one side, the scandalmongering of the newspaper that is hungry to expand its profits by having captured the decisive moment of the incident; on the other, the steamrolling character of power to crack down without mercy on everyone who rebels against it.

This has become a very concretely political discussion, but I have intentionally cited this episode at length because I think it perfectly symbolizes the situation of technical images in today's information era. It reveals the thinking of the authorities that everything shown in a technical image is the truth, the existence of the mass media which itself believes that all technical images (and probably articles as well) are documents of things that actually happened—and, further, the mass media's commodification of the document by making the masses believe all this too. Finally—and this is what allows the mass media to manipulate the situation—there is an unhappy love triangle between these three actors: the mass media is ultimately like hand and glove with the authorities, while the belief of the masses in the document only stabilizes the authorities. Looking at these photographs divorced from any context, I myself strongly feel the danger of all too easily slipping into the belief that they show a "crime scene." A kind of mass self-hypnosis comes about when a photograph is published through the mass media. The masses, who are isolated from dramatic reality, and only given a schedule of unskilled labor and simple leisure, believe that drama only exists on the other side of the cathode-ray tube or the newspaper photograph. Not even that—we immediately grasp that everything on the tube is an "incident," or something dramatic. I can offer another personal experience here. At the beginning of the year, one of my friends was suddenly arrested as a suspect in an incident. That day, his arrest was covered on television, and his house was shown as it was being searched. On the tube, this house where I had often visited looked like a place where someone truly heinous would live. This self-hypnosis wields almost astonishing power. One-sided values and morals start to impose themselves just from being arrested and having this broadcast.

At the beginning of this article, I wrote that the document has turned into a monument, and that the exhibition value of technical images has once again transformed into cult value. However, as I see it, these things all emerge from the naive view that technical images are documents and that everything documented in them has actually happened. This produces two uncritical attitudes within us. First is the attitude that everything actually documented in a technical image is reality, and that anything that is not documented is not reality. Second—and this is of course closely related to the first—is an uncritical attitude toward the fact that the mass media entirely controls the choice of whether to display a document or not, how to compose the context of a fragmentary document, and all of the other factors that determine its meaning. The masses simply believe what is given to them, and have turned into passive and uncritical receivers. To go even further, they are no longer the subject of history, but have been swapped out to become bystanders of history. Still, individual images are always only "half-manufactured," so their meaning is always malleable, depending on how they are combined. This is the decisive characteristic of technical images. For example, through a few additions and cuts, it would probably be quite simple to turn a Nazi propaganda film into an antifascist agitation film. The example of the *Yomiuri Shimbun* photographs from the November 11 Okinawa General Strike is an extremely primitive, drastic example of this.

To speak in terms of the situation of the technical images that surround us, all of the documentary images that pass through the mass media have been manipulated, and because of this, it is actually fair to claim that they are nothing more than illusions. Because these illusions go beyond mere illusion to compose a new reality, many difficulties remain before us.

This by no means ends with the kind of concrete political manipulation that I have described. If that were the case, I think things would actually be surprisingly easy. Arming ourselves, we must stake everything on exposing the manipulation of the mass media and developing countermanipulations to oppose it. Obviously, I may be taking things too lightly to put it like this. Even running that risk, on principle, our only tactical question should be how to counterattack against the attack of the enemy.

But the root of the situation goes even deeper, because our sensations are commandeered on a deeper level each day. Just consider technical images and vision alone. In our everyday lives, we are surrounded by countless technical images: images of sex, starting with nudes and pinup photos, product advertising photography, images about fashion, trends, and customs, and then all manner of broadly social imagery, which is not necessarily draped in political colors. They are fed to us every day, as a single stereotyped vision. What are they, anyway? Through their endless repetition, have we gradually become able to see the world only in accordance with this systematized vision? Andy Warhol has said that "repetition is what makes you famous," but this statement should not be written off as mere sophistry. It is much more incisive than that: it opposes the mechanism of today's information society, and inverts it in a critical and ironical way. Just as Alain Jouffroy says, politics is not just about students fighting police, or the speeches of presidents. It starts when the woman you love goes out to buy new curtains for the apartment she's moving in to with a new man, and you recognize her retreating figure from a distance. Politics first emerges from the totality of everyday life, which it then envelops.

Actually, I think the mass media of today's information society acts out its truly political role within the boundlessness of everyday life. The mass media systematizes everyday life and, through this, systematizes and controls our senses. Whatever potential for violence that sex has is nipped in the bud by the stereotyped view forced on us that keeps sex and commodities in their proper place. Just look at the nude photographs that fill the weekly magazines, week after week, or the recent television commercials full of sex. On the whole, they are all of a single type, and we look at these naked women as if we were looking at the photographs in a catalog of new sports cars. Words like "sexy" suggest nothing more than an extremely healthy and harmless kind of sex, in which all in the world is at peace. With this in mind, the issue of whether or not pubic hair appears in a photograph is entirely trivial. The same goes for pornography: once it is understood that it will not produce any cracks in the overall structure of society, it will be set free like lifting a ban on the fishing of sweetfish. But lifting a ban on pornography has nothing to do with the liberation of sex. Even if a magazine could publish a full-frontal photograph of sexual intercourse, this ban would have been lifted precisely because the photograph was, in the end, organized into a systematized vision.

These technical images that we come into contact with so frequently are manipulated, in the proper sense of the word. For example, even if a nude photograph is a document of the woman who modeled for it, it is unmistakably an illusion in the sense of its manipulated and controlled vision.

An illusion is just that, an illusion—it is absolutely not reality. Or rather, an illusion has its political basis in diverting our eyes away from reality. The manipulation of technical images by the state and the mass media has become this deep and this broad, so the idea that technical images are manipulated should be understood from such depth and breadth.

Of course, all manner of journalistic photographs—for example those showing atrocities like the recent bombing of North Vietnam, or the acts of terror committed by the Pakistani army against the

Bangladeshi independence movement—are no exception. In each case, these photographs are split off from their true meaning and rearranged within a completely different context. Through various kinds of information, we already know about American aggressions and atrocities in Vietnam to the point of exhaustion. But the fissure between our knowledge of these atrocities and our ability to bring them to an end is clear to anyone. Without question, the mass media's manipulation of information plays a large role here. For example, when something is framed by "the issue of the Vietnam War"—or when the tragic figure of a young girl affected by pollution is framed by "the issue of pollution"—it is placed within parentheses and rapidly estranged from our reality. This, too, can be called manipulation of information.

The photographs that we photographers take and display are also not free from the manipulation of the mass media. And not just even that—the many technical images that we produce day after day become the raw material for that manipulation and thus become commodities. This is already obvious. Is it possible to escape from it? To continue to take and display photographs without asking oneself this question obviously means assisting the other side. Asking oneself this question must become the minimum requirement for anyone who chooses to be a conscious photographer, or who undertakes to be an artist working with images. Day after day, through the manipulation of the mass media, the photographs that we take are incorporated as illusions, remanufactured products daubed with reality. Or, we could quit being photographers, quit being image producers. This, too, would be a harsh way of life, one more like death. In deeply political cases, such as that of the reporting around the Okinawa protest, if it is not even possible to protect one's own film through effort and thought, the act of photographing is already a form of assisting power.[13] This situation continues to clearly manifest itself today. The indefinite stance of the uncommitted amateur photographers and university photo club members who flock to protests form a Private Photographic Evidence Squad for the state. Enzensberger points out that in today's capitalist and socialist countries alike, the mass media's manipulation is connected to power. At the same time, he also writes that in a free socialist system, the media can fully manifest its own productive capabilities, which only becomes possible when the mass is both sender and receiver, and can organize itself within a socialized form of learning. This is of course correct as far as it goes, but it is only possible within a classless society, after the true revolution to come. On this point, Enzensberger's schema sounds somewhat utopian. There are obviously innumerable difficulties on the way to this revolution, and the mass media cannot be considered as a problem that is separate from the dynamics of social revolution in general.

Frantz Fanon has analyzed the meaning of the woman's haik (a garment that covers the face), the radio, and French language in the various stages of the Algerian revolution. Here, I will focus on the radio and French in particular. In the first stage of revolution, listening to the radio and hearing French meant lending an ear to the entirety of the colonists and colonial authorities' values, which were intertwined with the French language. To protect their ethnic identity, Algerians rejected the radio and the French language, narrowly managing to avoid being dismantled. In the second stage, since all information was controlled by the French government and the colonial authorities, it became necessary for the Algerians to know how their struggles were progressing for themselves. Once they set up the Voice of Fighting Algeria, they started to organize their own language.[14] In the third stage, they used this broadcast for French, too, in order to preserve the validity of communication. These developments precisely correspond with each stage of armed class struggle. The important thing here is the process, which happens in reality, through which one set of values is sublated by another.

"Looked upon as a transmission belt of the colonialist power, as a means in the hands of the occupier by which to maintain his strangle hold on the nation, the radio was frowned upon. Before 1954, switching on the radio meant giving asylum to the occupier's words; it meant allowing the colonizer's language to filter into the very heart of the house, the last of the supreme bastions of the national spirit."[15] Then, in 1955, the first radio broadcasts not in French started. Needless to say, the French jammed these radio waves many times, so the Voice of Fighting Algeria often countered this by changing its frequency. For this reason, there was no guarantee that the entirety of a broadcast could be heard by the entire Algerian people. Listeners had to assemble whatever fragmented information they could, and put together the true meaning of the information for themselves through group discussions. Fanon's description of this process is quite moving. But the point is that the problem of the mass media and the way to resolve it can only be discussed within a concrete political process. The problem of the mass media is deeply connected to the question of politics—from its apex in narrowly defined notions of "the political," to the vast domain of everyday life which supports it.

To conclude, let me state the problem clearly once more. Today, we live in the midst of illusions produced by the myth that technical images are documents. These illusions are extremely political, precisely because we live in an age in which nothing can avoid being political. Everything must start with us rejecting these illusions and working to drag out each and every myth inside of us into the light. Of course, this also includes the enlightening work of using language to critique the deception of technical images, not by claiming that documents are straight reflections of reality, but that they can be transformed in any way through the preparations of their sender. The case of something like the *Yomiuri Shimbun* frame-up in Okinawa demands that we strike back concretely.

At the same time, we producers of images have been handed a difficult task of living out a paradox. In other words, we have to use images themselves, through the mass media itself, to draw out the mass media's manipulation and how that logic appears in the social manifestations of technical images. It is already possible to see attempts of this sort in Pop artists' "re-signification of the sign." By experimenting with magnifying halftone dots (Roy Lichtenstein) or obsessively repeating the same image (Andy Warhol's Marilyn Monroes), their images undoubtedly explode the structure of the image itself and puncture its falsehood. Then there is the method known as hyperrealism, which has rapidly gained prominence over the past two years. This method looks at the world photographically and depicts subjects in accordance with the camera's vision; in this way, it shows us, if by accident, how much our own vision is being transformed by modeling itself on the vision of mass media. Finally, in film, Jean-Luc Godard's *Wind from the East* and *Weekend* persistently voice the critique that technical images are not reality; if one thinks one sees blood on screen, the films themselves suggest that this is actually nothing more than red ink, and that images are fictions that borrow the appearance of reality. Here, we can easily recall Godard's deliberate "inside jokes," in which people often appear in his films saying that this is a film, not reality.

Clearly, our battle lines span two domains. First, there is the domain of the concrete and political manipulation of information by power, and second, there is the home turf of Enzensberger's "consciousness industry"—the daily manipulation and exploitation of our consciousness and our senses, which deeply permeate our everyday lives. However much we can strike back concretely, these are our two fronts. Of course, these are both rooted in the relations between people, so ours must be a political battle.

First published in the art magazine *Bijutsu Techō*, July 1972. Later collected in *Why an Illustrated Botanical Guide? Collected Writings on Images by Takuma Nakahira* (Shōbunsha, 1973).

Notes

1 This sentence illustrates the range of media that are included in the word *eizō* (see page 21, n. 1), which Nakahira uses throughout this essay.

2 Hans Magnus Enzensberger (1929–2022) was a German poet and critic. In February 1972, he visited Tokyo for a symposium held in his honor, where Nakahira was one of the discussants.

3 Hans Magnus Enzensberger, "Constituents of a Theory of the Media," *New Left Review*, no. 64 (November 1, 1970): 34–35. Emphasis by Nakahira. Nakahira cites the Japanese translation by Kōji Nakano, published in the August 1971 issue of the journal *Bungei*. To capture the specific nuances of the Japanese translation that Nakahira draws upon, the original English translation has been modified slightly.

4 In February 1972, police chased a militant left-wing organization across the mountains of Gunma and Nagano, a few hours' drive from Tokyo. Some members of the group were arrested, while five members fled to the resort town of Karuizawa, where they took a hostage in a building called Asama Lodge and holed themselves up against a protracted police siege.

5 At the time that Nakahira was writing, the trial and fallout from the incident was still in progress. In time, it emerged that fourteen of the group's twenty-nine members were killed as part of internal purges.

6 A volume of essays by the German critic Walter Benjamin (1892–1940) was translated into Japanese in 1965, several years before a similar volume appeared in English.

7 This is an excerpt of Nakahira's 1969 essay, "What Does It Mean to Be Contemporary?," published across the May–August 1969 issues of the magazine *Design*, and later republished in *For a Language to Come* (1970).

8 Here, Nakahira uses the well-known terms of the Swiss linguist Ferdinand de Saussure (1857–1913).

9 Around the time Nakahira wrote this essay, articles in Japanese photography magazines often described the photographs published in *Provoke* in terms of *are bure* ("rough grain, blurriness") or *bure boke* ("blurriness, out-of-focus"). *Provoke* is still associated with these terms today, even in English-language discourse, lending credence to Nakahira's sardonic claim. *Provoke* members did not invent these terms, much less these photographic techniques.

10 This phrase was the title of a roundtable discussion with Yutaka Takanashi, Nakahira, Kineo Kuwabara, and others in the April 1969 issue of *Asahi Camera*. *Conpora*, an abbreviation of *contemporary*, refers to a mode of snapshot photography with a particular focus on the banality of everyday life. It was the subject of much discussion at this time, and both Nakahira and Kōji Taki criticized it in print.

11 Enzensberger, "Constituents of a Theory of the Media," 18–19.

12 On October 7, 1974, Yū Matsunaga was found guilty and sentenced to one year in prison and two additional years of a suspended sentence. Matsunaga won his innocence on appeal in 1976, and later successfully sued the government for wrongful damages. In Japanese legal history, the trial itself has come to be known as the "Image Trial." Matsunaga had

traveled to Okinawa in 1971 to study the traditional dyeing art of *bingata*; at the time of writing, he continues his practice as a dyeing artist.

13 Nakahira is referencing the case of Kō Yoshioka, a mainland photographer who supported and photographed the demonstration. As part of the Matsunaga case, police officers forcibly entered Yoshioka's home, and seized his film. This event drew media attention, and Yoshioka successfully sued the government for damages.

14 The Voice of Fighting Algeria was a clandestine radio station established in 1956 by the National Liberation Front, a political party that fought for Algeria's independence from French rule.

15 Frantz Fanon, "This Is the Voice of Algeria," in *A Dying Colonialism*, trans. Haakon Chevalier (New York: Grove Press, 1967), 92.

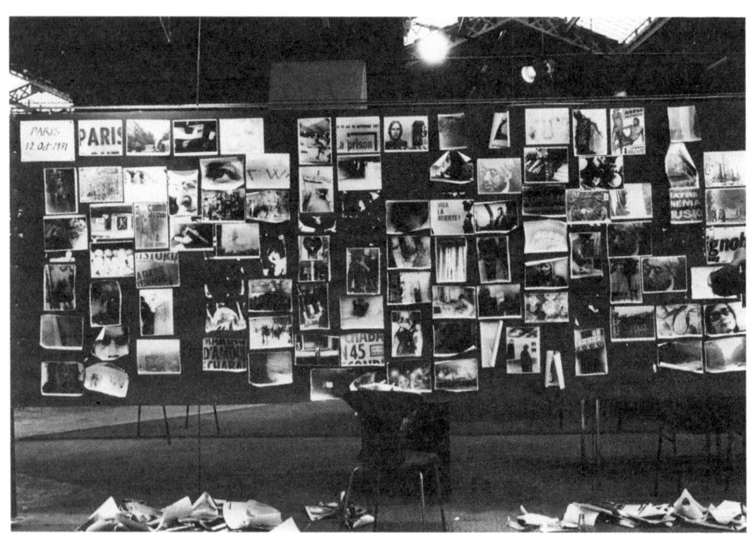

Takuma Nakahira, *Untitled*, from the series *Circulation: Date, Place, Events*, 1971

Why Jazz Now?
Preface to a Theory of Place

1

Last year, I participated in two exhibitions and found myself involved with the world of contemporary art. The first was the 10th Contemporary Art Exhibition of Japan, which opened in Tokyo last May (1971); the other was the 7th Paris Biennale, held last September. For the former, I agreed to show my work, found myself at my wit's end after wasting three months, made a big show of talking about being damned if I did and damned if I didn't, and finally withdrew from the exhibit. With the latter, too, I came close to quitting, but at the last minute the commissioner, my friend Takahiko Okada, *admonished* me, so I said why not and headed to Paris, with the secondary purpose of doing some sightseeing. As for the outcome, there was nothing worth writing here: it's already old news. But through these two opportunities, I came into contact with contemporary art for the first time. I'm not sure whether it is meaningful for me to write down now what I felt then. But the problems I encountered were hardly unique to contemporary art; they are problems common to all of us who are forced to live in this age. Such problems seem to be a condition of our life that seeps out from the core of our "situation" (this word is now so overused that it's as worthless and empty as a blank check passed around from hand to hand, and yet, even so,

I dare to use it . . .) such that even as I make these complaints, I find myself on the verge of drowning, struggling to keep my head above water. That being the case, it is clear that I have no choice but to start with a consideration of the pressing circumstances of the here and now.

Of course, because I am a photographer, I have never had an especially deep interest in art in general, much less contemporary art. But fools rush in where angels fear to tread, so let me use the privilege of the amateur and state what I thought I saw clearly in the major trends of contemporary art, as represented by conceptual art: the figure of knowledge, a knowledge that stood off entirely on its own, stripped of any connection to reality and spinning around in empty circles. In other words, what I witnessed there were attempts at boring ever deeper and more narrowly into the infinitesimal, all driven by a neurotic sensibility. No—that's not quite right, either. These were not attempts to grasp reality more clearly by focusing on the infinitesimal (which, as the phrase "one-point perspective" suggests, can undoubtedly serve as an important method of recognition). While at first glance the work I saw might have appeared to do this, in fact it brought about the phenomenon of a knowledge that gradually abandons all relation to a given reality, repeating a series of self-propelled operations to emerge in the inverted form of a knowledge-for-knowledge's sake. One-point perspective can be a valid method for acquiring a deeper grasp on reality, as long as the energy focused on the single point is equal to the energy of the feedback generated by the corresponding total reality. But what I saw was nothing like this. On the contrary, it was nothing more than a competition to produce the most neurotic *convulsions* of knowledge, and further, to make them socially fashionable. It was like watching an intellectual sleight of hand. Sleight of hand relies on a preestablished harmony: there is always some trick at play, but in order to enjoy the show, everyone implicitly agrees ahead of time to forget about that. It is exactly the same in contemporary art, as represented by so-called conceptual art. What is matter, they ask, or what is the concept of the human—and then they test these questions to an infinitesimal degree. And yet, when we ask what purpose all this is for, the individual artists who pursue these questions seem to lack any connection whatsoever to reality. Yes, matter is matter. And humans are humans. We have to grant this distinction. But our modern history has made the relation between these terms vague, personifying things to match the image of the human, and coloring the world in anthropomorphic tones. Modern humanism was just this sort of thing, and more concretely, modern science was created to compel the world to submit to the human. But in the end, modern science gave birth to war, and to the grave reality of pollution that today covers the entire planet. This alone is enough to declare that modern humanism is bankrupt. Still, that recognition only acquires meaning within the lives we each lead as individuals living through this age, and everything will surely be settled up within our individual lives. A recognition that misses this point is only recognition for recognition's sake. Such recognition and its illustrations (in other words, works of contemporary art) are utterly meaningless. Albert Camus once wrote: "Galileo, who held a scientific truth of great importance, abjured it with the greatest ease as soon as it endangered his life. In a certain sense, he did right. That truth was not worth the stake. Whether the earth or the sun revolves around the other is a matter of profound indifference. To tell the truth, it is a futile question. On the other hand, I see many people die because they judge that life is not worth living."[1]

But my purpose in this essay is not to comment on contemporary art. Instead, I want to speak of the general condition of today's era, in which knowledge is losing its connection to reality. This is not limited to the field of art, but extends to everything that we call "thought," including photography, which I am involved in, and also jazz.

"The boring of knowledge"—does such a phrase even exist? In economics, there is a term called the "boring phenomenon." It refers to a case in which a variety of small parasitical subindustries arise around a single central industry—the more complex the state of contemporary capitalism, the more numerous they will be—and gouge out small holes in it. Take the example of film production. To make a film, you need a crew and cameras. But a film can't be produced with these alone. You also need audio and lighting gear, and then you need someone to transport this fragile lighting equipment. From this emerges not a generalized shipping industry, but a specialized one, handling only lighting equipment. From the film director down to the lighting equipment shipping specialists, everyone contributes to the movie under production. Yes, the director is responsible for the film. But the lighting equipment shipping specialist is responsible only for safely shipping the lighting equipment. He has no relation whatsoever to the contents of the movie in question. The same sort of phenomenon can be seen in the situation of knowledge, which seems to be completely absorbed into a single aspect of some object, boring deeper and deeper into that one tiny aspect. It's like the situation of a honeybee that plunges its head into the fruit that is richest in nectar, and, in its single-minded pursuit of this nectar, burrows down until its entire body disappears. Naturally, at this moment the honeybee does not grasp the totality of the fruit. In the same way, a knowledge engrossed in the process of boring deeper and deeper into a single point fails to grasp the world or reality in its entirety. In fact, for such purposes, even a hazy view of some totality would be a hindrance. This is because, for our honeybee, the nectar constitutes the entirety of the fruit; the lush flesh of the fruit, which contains the nectar, is of almost no interest.

In a certain sense, to focus on a single point and dig into it ever more sharply may guarantee the healthy development of knowledge. Criticism or negation directed at a single point can generate new hypotheses, which in turn can lead to further criticism and negation, and this unending chain can deepen knowledge. It is also true that such knowledge, by limiting itself to the particular, can actually help, little by little, to clarify the totality of the world. Knowledge, after all, consists primarily not of contents that are obtained, but rather of the attempt to know.

But if this boring is too small and too deeply drilled, and it eventually loses not just its connection to totality, but even its ability to be reduced to totality, what meaning would knowledge have? I wrote above that knowledge has less to do with content, and more to do with "the attempt to know." Even so, hasn't this sort of attempt given up on achieving any result at all? But the fact that we are alive means that we are alive in reality. How does knowledge relate to this? It seems that today we live in an age in which only neurotic *convulsions*, the tinier the better, are regarded as having any value. And aren't the questions about what knowledge is for, and why we attempt to know things, gradually becoming more vague? When the connection of these infinitesimal problems to totality goes unquestioned, and when they become part of society without any mediation, they become trends lacking any of the essential purpose of knowledge and, as with all trends, they become commodified.

The works I saw at the two exhibitions of contemporary art were more or less of this nature. Of course, there must have been some exceptions. But on the whole, I feel that this is the main current supporting contemporary art today.

The important thing is that with each advance in this boring of knowledge, knowledge itself gradually loses touch with the reality in which we live.

2

My essay seems to have taken a grandiose turn since its opening. To tell the truth, I have no idea how to link the above discussion to my assigned topic of a "Preface to a Theory of Place" nor, for that matter, to jazz. What in the world do I know about jazz anyway? To get back on track, perhaps I should describe my own personal connection to jazz. About ten years ago, I had graduated university and (even though the Anpo struggle was long lost) was unable to escape the sense of drifting I experienced in the student movement.[2] Out of the corner of my eye, I watched my more cheerful friends adjust and move on, while I was filled with insatiable desire yet seemingly unable to pull the trigger. That's when I first encountered modern jazz, which was gradually gaining popularity at the time; I'm pretty sure it happened at Duet, a tiny jazz café that reeked of piss. The room was dimly lit, and the spoiled, depressed young men around my age who filled the place, looking like their stomachs were upset, would sit crouched over, as if physically weighed down by the pounding reverberations that came from the ceiling. To my eyes, it looked more like they were enduring rather than enjoying the sounds. This was the atmosphere in which I first encountered jazz. I came to know Thelonious Monk, distant and transparent and inorganic like raindrops, and Miles Davis, who had a swing that just rolled along; I came to know the straight-ahead rhythm of Art Blakey. But it wasn't a matter of any specific musicians. For me, the totality of the rhythm pounded out by Black or White jazz musicians was something entirely new. In the vacuum that characterized that age, it was as if I had become matter itself, and like my peers, I immersed myself in the pleasure of passively surrendering myself to be swallowed up into that mass of sound. I remember frequenting modern jazz cafés for about two years after that. There was Mama by the Yaesu exit of Tokyo Station, 69 on the Kyōbashi side of Ginza, Dig in Shinjuku, and Oscar and Arinko in Shibuya. In those days, I flitted from job to job, never staying long at any: two days as a television announcer, one month boxing up transistor radios, stints as a translator for a foreign news agency and as an editor at a general magazine affiliated with the New Left. One way or another, the locations of these jazz cafés were all connected to those jobs.

I have no idea if those cafés are still around today. But looking back on those days, the truth is that music, and in particular modern jazz, presented what seemed like an unrealizable dream, one so incredibly vivid that I was almost frightened to touch it, even as it was so far away: the experience of giving myself over to directness, which the corporeal language of jazz offered up. At the very least, jazz gave me the intoxication of passivity.

André Gide said that "all arts aspire toward music," yet on the other hand I think it was Salvador Dalí who said, "Music soothes people's hearts. It calms people's hearts. For this reason, all music is reactionary."[3] I have no idea which is correct. Probably both. That is because if something is so enchanting as to make us forget reality, then it must be worth aspiring to. At any rate, back then jazz for me seemed closer to the latter description. Later, when I became a magazine editor and got addicted to watching movies and writing film criticism, and still later when I got into photography, jazz gradually faded into the background.

It is only quite recently that I have come back into contact with jazz. By chance, I became acquainted with the jazz vocalist Minami Yasuda, and for the first time I started to attend live performances by Japanese jazz musicians. Up until then, the only Japanese jazz musicians whose names I knew were the likes of Terumasa Hino and Sadao Watanabe; in my infantile knowledge, I used to lump all the Japanese musicians together as simple imitators of Black jazz musicians. This was nothing but a prejudice arising from sheer ignorance. But then I started listening to Minami Yasuda's powerful shout, and I became familiar with the likes of Isao Suzuki and Masabumi Kikuchi.

They were either around my age or, more often, considerably younger than me. And they were a different breed from the sort of people I had associated with previously. It's not just that they had a different attitude toward life. More than anything, they had a distinct method of language, a language of the flesh, or perhaps a gestural language. I had only been familiar with spoken and written language, so to encounter them produced a shock, almost like encountering an alien race. Quite shy and awkward in ordinary conversation, once they stepped onto stage it was as if they were reborn as new people: the rhythms they pounded out and the words they shouted asserted themselves one by one, giving off a brilliance beyond anything that spoken or written language could attain. Of course, I could not fully discern their individual differences or levels of talent. But without question, a new language was there, a language more closely connected to flesh. It was, in other words, a language lived out by flesh.

3

Just now, I said that most Japanese jazz musicians are simply imitators of American jazz players, Black or White. It's certainly true that Japan does not have a great deal of what you could call original jazz. Most players will copy an American number and rearrange it according to their own personal style. Does this guarantee that the level of Japanese jazz will be low? Hardly. Isn't it the case that originality has been excessively worshipped in our world? Haven't we been too prone to fetishize "creation" and "creativity" as sacred ideas? This is most clearly manifested in the boring of knowledge I discussed above. Out of a desire to be original or individual, we end up pouring everything into the task of boring down into tiny holes of personal style. We mistake the convulsions of terminal nerves for creativity and individuality. The logic permeating all of this is the logic of competition, of elbowing others out—that is to say, the logic of capitalist free market competition. Of course, we try to string words together, moving ever forward. But we still need to grapple with the question of whether the last, most advanced word articulated through this process brings us to a deeper grasp of reality.

With its directness, it seems to me that by its very nature, jazz might hack away at such knowledge, from the side as it were. This way of putting it might represent a reactionary belief, an infantile superstition about jazz that links it to Blackness and Africa and sets it up as a distant shore to yearn after, pining for *something that isn't here*. This motif of thought, or affective pattern, shows up with great frequency and in many different guises among members of the tribe known as intellectuals. Its reactionary nature is revealed most clearly in the political and intellectual realms. We see it, for example, in the unmediated yearning for the Third World or, closer to home, in offhand responses to the all-out resistance mounted by the United Red Army at the Asama Lodge to the effect that "they fought all too well."[4] These instances demonstrate what should properly be called "historical reaction," because the speakers project themselves onto a distant shore, and in doing so completely cast aside the reality that they are actually living. Incidentally, this sort of affective pattern can be called catharsis, a word that shares the same Greek etymological root with intestinal catarrh and chronic gastric catarrh. In other words, it involves something that flows through us without being fully digested. I'm getting sidetracked again, but insofar as we're talking about jazz, I might well be one of those suffering from intestinal catarrh. Having acknowledged this, I'd like to offer a little more consideration of "place," the assigned theme of this essay.

For me, this is intimately related to the questions of what we mean by two terms: "to create," and "language." This returns to the question that I raised somewhat abstractly at the outset: whether "to create" can have any meaning in this era in which, under our current mode of knowledge, "to create" means nothing more than a single-minded self-concealment. "Creation," which properly should take its beginning from reality and then return to that reality for verification, has now abandoned that circuit and instead spins in empty circles. This is necessarily connected to another question: What is language for us, and what does it mean to create in language?

We've been speaking about our distrust of language, about the fruitlessness of words, for a long time now. There has probably never been an age that insists so rigorously on verifying language as ours. And yet, this of course does not lead to the conclusion that we should ignore language, nor does it result in the invention of new, fresher language. This is because language cannot be invented like a toy, and also because nothing else can replace language, not even technical images. That is because language is consciousness itself.

At this point, I'm unqualified to say anything about rhythm in jazz. I suppose it's possible to convert rhythm into words, but that sort of linear treatment would require a more meticulous consideration than I can provide. Leaving that for later, here I would like to think a little bit about language in songs, about the meaning that each word has within the context of a song's lyrics.

I have a reference on this matter in front of me. Let me try quoting from it: "On the contrary, we could say that commonplaces are, in a sense, the place where we see a constant, obstinate attempt to create words. Linguists have occasionally searched (without success) for the origin of language. But there is one kind of language which, *at every moment*, originates before our very eyes—or at least tries to do so. . . . I happily accept that sayings give anyone who hears them uncharitably the impression of a phrase that is repeated at random. But, conversely, the person uttering them discovers with joy the many thousands of ingenious applications that the expressions 'Do you realize,' 'Goodbye and thank you,' and 'All you have to do is . . .' lend themselves to with the same sense of happiness."[5] This passage comes from Jean Paulhan's *The Flowers of Tarbes*.

The lyrics a jazz vocalist sings are determined in advance by the songwriter. In that sense, it's possible to say that they are the creation of the songwriter, not of the singer who sings them. But can we really draw such a one-sided conclusion? On the contrary, isn't it a question of to what degree, within a given "place," a singer rediscovers their own language, at that time and on that spot? Creation is absolutely not about making something out of nothing. How you live out your given "place," or the "place" you have chosen for yourself: *that* is creation.

First published in the Japanese magazine *Jazz*, May 1972. Later collected in *Why an Illustrated Botanical Guide? Collected Writings on Images by Takuma Nakahira* (Shōbunsha, 1973).

Notes

1 Albert Camus, "An Absurd Reasoning," from *The Myth of Sisyphus*, trans. Justin O'Brien (New York: Knopf, 1955), 3–4.

2 As a university student, Nakahira participated in demonstrations held in Tokyo in 1960 against the US-Japan Security Treaty, which guaranteed a United States military presence in Japan. Hundreds of thousands of people took to the streets of Tokyo to protest against the signing of this treaty, which is commonly known by its abbreviated name in Japanese, "Anpo."

3 The first quotation may be Nakahira misidentifying Walter Pater's aphorism, "All art constantly aspires toward the condition of music." The translators have been unable to identify the source of the second quotation.

4 For more information about the Asama Lodge, see the essay in this volume, "The Illusion Called Document: From Document to Monument," page 36.

5 Jean Paulhan, *The Flowers of Tarbes or, Terror in Literature*, trans. Michael Syrotinski (Urbana: University of Illinois Press, 2006), 48–49.

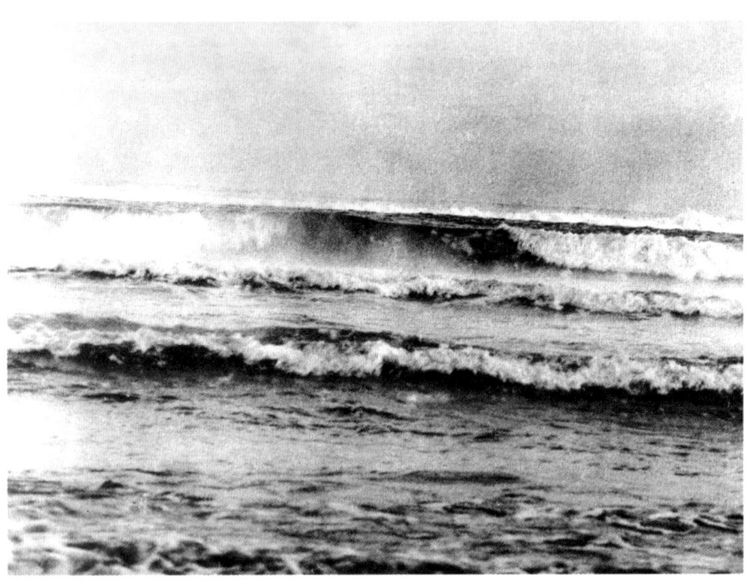

Takuma Nakahira, *Untitled*, from the photobook *For a Language to Come*, 1970

Why an Illustrated Botanical Guide?

1

Perhaps this is a little sudden. But I want to begin this text with a tentative personal response to a critical letter to the editor written by a relatively young reader about one of my essays ("The Illusion Called Document: From Document to Monument") published in a certain magazine.[1] I want to think about why I've spent almost no time with the work of taking photographs over the past couple of years, and so much more time thinking about the social foundation that photography produces as media, or, to put it a little more personally, this is so I can confirm for myself why I am no longer able to take photographs as I did before. One could say that this criticism was made with good intentions. It was a criticism directed at the loss of the poesy that was once in my photographs, and also at my own shift toward becoming a verbose critic, as if to fill that gap. Of course, I admit to some of the things that were pointed out. Still, I also know that I can no longer return to the world of poesy and images [*imēji*].[2] This is because I firmly believe that even if I were to possess an extremely intimate personal feeling toward poesy and images, precisely because of such feeling, clinging to them is something that I would have to reject in and of itself. At this point, I ask the letter writer to allow me to quote his brief letter.

This is something I think about every time I come into contact with your writing. The more verbose you get, the more you try to capture what you call your own thought, doesn't your truth seem to recede, away from your body, ever further into the distance?

I have no connection to your acrobatic analyses of art, which seem to pick out every last detail. However, even I can point out the photographs that resonate, in some time or other, with the soundboard in my heart.

I once felt poetry in scenes of seashores that you had captured. Deep within my heart, there was a feeling like waves cresting and breaking. . . .

"What is possible for a camera is no more than to make simple records as some enumeration of a hodgepodge of different phenomena that happen before one's eyes, a reality whose relation to the totality is not even clear. Still, because this is an object before one's eyes, it can hold reality."[3] After saying this, you built up records of your own life through photography. A vulgar judgment has no power in and of itself, but there was no lie in your passion, through which you couldn't but voice these concerns. Such a thought may be fickle and vague, but within the sigh emitted from the depths of your spirit there lurks something worthy of belief. All the same, haven't you now exchanged that sigh for a flood of elegant prose? Now, you say: "My claim that photographs are documents was an antithesis of the prevailing theories of this type."[4] This state of affairs is cleanly settled. When you entrusted the evidence of your own life to the documents of photography, this was already full of contradictions. In the contaminated word *document*, I could see that you were sticking to your antithesis with all your might. No matter what form your self-critique took, I can hardly say that anything remarkable emerged from it. . . .

Now, against the ground of your own thought, you are trying to construct for your photographs a poisoned meaning through a poisoned language. In the pathos-like emotion felt when something is lost, there is some vague beauty, but there is also unmistakably something sad.

I can still clearly hear the relentless din of waves.[5]

How in the world should I respond to this critique? Should I agree with him and lament the loss of "poetry" in my photography? Or would it be better to hit back with an even more high-handed attitude, and construct "a poisoned meaning through a poisoned language"? True, I admit that what the writer calls the "poetry" of my photographs has disappeared. And I also admit that I have not yet shown any photographs to take their place.

But it seems that the problem is not so simple as the mere disappearance of "poetry," or the vanishing of poesy. What is this thing that we have grown used to calling "poetry"? Couldn't it be a synonym for the "image" that connects me to the world? Arguably, there are few words used so broadly yet with such imprecision as this word, "image." However, isn't what the writer calls "poetry" an image that says the world must be like so, one that says the world must be this way ahead of time, an image already decided? Isn't this a priori "image" that I capture something that, in concrete terms, appears as a world that I have embellished and sentimentalized? That is to say, doesn't it turn the world into a reflection of my own loose impression of "my desires, the shadow of my convictions," and unilaterally refuse to show the world as it is? If that is the case, then "poetry" is born precisely in the zone of ambiguity where the shore of myself and the world that is fulfilled as itself murkily dissolve into one another. There, through emotionalization, I unmistakably turn the world into private property.

Since publishing a photobook about two years ago, I have not been able to do anything, and I have not even made an effort to do anything.[6] I have started to sense that the reason for this is the fact that doubts about precisely these words, "poetry" and "image," started to appear within me—dimly at first, but gradually with more clarity. At the same time, there is certainly a distant but firm connection to what I have just said, concerning what the writer calls my "worthless self-criticism." I have the premonition that I cannot take photographs except in a form that includes a critique of photography as a social mode of expression, and that if photography is a language itself, then perhaps the only thing demanded of photographers working in the field of expression is to produce a meta-language of photography that incorporates self-critique. It is said that this is the age of the technical image [*eizō*], and we live surrounded by untold numbers of them. But instead of saying that they carry out their intrinsic function as technical images—to be signs that indicate reality—we should perhaps say that they themselves form a second reality, which we would have to call a pseudo-reality. They are not reality, but they constantly force our gaze toward fabrications that have been daubed with reality. This is what I called (in the essay that the letter writer criticized) "systematized vision." Clearly, its political role is to turn our eyes away from reality and systematically fix them on a space that is not really there. As I discussed above, this is less related to the dimension of manipulating the world in the image of personal desire. Instead, it is a more concrete problem at a political and social level, and it leads to a fundamental question: within such a reality, in which the impetus for the critique of reality has been removed, is it really possible for any photographer working as an "expressor" to exist without any skepticism of the act of continuing to take and exhibit photographs, no matter what form they take? But this is something I will address later. For now, I would like to limit the discussion solely to that which is called "image," or what the letter writer calls "poetry."

For a long time, "image" or "poetry" has been taken for granted as something to expect from works of art. We are all too familiar with the fact that, whatever their form, works have been criticized or rejected by saying that they have no image, or that their image is weak. Moreover, we have not cast any doubt on this situation, even for a moment. That is because "image" itself has guaranteed art as art. To put it in an extreme way, because "image" is the figure of the world that belongs to an artist, it must inhere a priori in that subject. This idea has been believed throughout modernity, beginning historically around the time of the Renaissance, when the subject first recognized itself; now, at long last, it is beginning to fall under some doubt. An artist was required to see and touch the world based on an a priori image. But in the end, this was based on the individual, and further, didn't it simply mean a distortion of the world, an anthropomorphizing of the world by the human? It is beyond doubt that we are standing at a historical crossroads in the present moment, forced to reflect deeply, at the level of society, as well as at the level of all of our thoughts and perceptions, about this fact. For example, although technology was developed to make the world into a tool for human use, the result is that it now antagonizes the human. Today, we can see that the world is definitely starting to rebel against the human's instrumentalization and anthropomorphization of the world. For the first time, the human kneels before the world.

The history of modernity sets up an absolute and binary opposition between the self and the world; following this schema, it has been the history of the self instrumentalizing and transforming the world according to its own desire, to human desire. Here, the image was the absolute king, the ruler. In this case, the word *image* could be rephrased as an a priori ideal or figure that depicts the world according to human thinking. It was presumed that the human would inevitably possess and capture the world. Still, there can be no debate that this was an idealistic reflection of an extremely limited historical age—the modern age, in which the individual reigned supreme. The world itself was an object of personal, individual desire; it was a thing to be subjugated. This recalls certain vulgar morals, like the accumulation of wealth and social climbing. This is the spirit of modern humanism, which privileges such ideas and ideals over the world as it is. Of course, the spirit of an age is bound to appear in art. Needless to say, modern art is a figure of the world projected onto the individual called the artist. Or no, even better—on the contrary, it is an image of the world being a particular way that the artist has had all along that the artist projects onto the world. This is the true form of what is called the image. We could say that the strength of a definite image is everything that is required of the artist, and that its technical externalization is the work, the act of expression. All manner of works are separated into the binary of content and form, and form actually constitutes works as works. Things like the style of literature, or the shape, line, and color of a painting are thought to be literal tools by which to exhibit the ideals of the creator. In other words, the image of the world that the individual artist has is prioritized above all else, and the most important thing is to ensure that this image matches up neatly with the respective images held by the many people who will see and come in contact with the work. This means that, as long as the work does not betray the preconceived ideas and schemas that those people have of reality, and does no more than explain them, the act of expression is complete.

But this is not looking at the world as it is; on the contrary, it means no more than closing one's eyes to the world. Our eyes, fixed within their sockets, turn inward. Actually, in this case, the only question is what figure the human, and in particular the artist as an individual, has of the world, no matter how much the world may be moving or changing. Standing before a work of art, observers have only one task: to unpack and understand through the work what kind of image the given artist has concealed there. Just as Alain Robbe-Grillet has said, the work is established here as "a grid or screen set with bits of different colored glass that fracture our field of vision into tiny assimilable facets."[7] This is no more than a closed circuit. This closed circuit does not ask how much of the world is there, operating solely—like solving a puzzle—through the verification of the relationship between the image of the world belonging to the artist and the image of the world belonging to those who come in contact with it. Either way, what connects these two is the conceited, human-centric thought that arises from the idea that the world can be subjugated to the human, that it can be colored and manipulated according to the way that humans imagine it.

Now, however, the world is truly betraying the ideas and images of the human, of artists; it is appearing as something that transcends them. The modern idea that the artist is the center of the world, or that the world is the self, is starting to collapse. Naturally, then, the view of art which holds that a work represents the artist's image is also inevitably shattering. Beyond the image of the self, there is always a world that appears as the world, and this process of unlimited "encounter" must replace our conventional artistic acts.[8] From this point on, our artistic task might be to make an absolute division, in which the world exists decisively as it is and the other shore exists decisively as the other shore. In a certain sense, this means admitting the defeat of the human by the world. Yet, insofar as history has already revealed that the idea of mixing our own shore with the other shore is no more than a deception, we clearly have no other point of departure than to desperately accept that defeat.

2

"That's cute," the man said. "That marmoset . . . "

"Sure, but it's mean," the woman said. "I remember that my grandmother used to have one. She was always giving it her best food. And do you think the thing appreciated her? Are you kidding? It bit her ear so hard that she bled! A truly awful beast!"

"It was probably trying to show her affection," the man said.

Adam was suddenly seized with the inexplicable desire to straighten everything out. He turned to the couple and explained.

"It's neither cute nor mean," he said. "It's a marmoset."[9]
(J. M. G. Le Clézio)

For me, "image" is already something to be overcome. This image that supposedly departs from me and unilaterally reaches the world, in the process distorting the world and coloring it with my own inclinations—now, inside of me, this image is being negated. It is not the case that the world and the self are linked by a unilateral, personal gaze. I exist through the gaze of things. It is facile to understand the human through the intellectual jargon that "world = interior = existence." There is only one direction toward which we should aim: thinking in accordance with concrete reality. As much as I may look at the world, it will always throw the gaze of things back to me at the same time. The world refuses my gaze; there is only the hard, "impermeable crust" of things.[10]

To see the inside of walls
Is not granted to us.
It is great to smash them,
Their facade is on display.[11]
(Eugène Guillevic)

And so, in this way, the world now spreads out before me (and behind me as well, of course) as a corporealized space. In the end, what is expression, and especially that method of expression called photography? Of course, it is not an expression or externalization of the self's image. That is precisely what photography is least suited for. Such externalization or expression of the image blocks the encounter between the self and world, in the truest sense of this phrase. To take a photograph is to organize the thought of things, the gaze of things. I do not ask a single photograph to be an image that symbolizes how I think the world is, or how I think it must be. A thing or a world that is already known can be described. But an unknown world extends out beyond here, and one can lie in wait, ready to receive the symbols that this world emits by chance (not to belabor the point, but it should go without saying that these symbols are the inverse of the symbols of the world's meaning that the self captures). Perhaps, in this way, photographic expression is first made possible through this joint effort between the thought of things and the thought of the self.

For this to happen, human projections onto the world and the personification of both things and the world must be completely eliminated. This is because our thought, in seeing everything in a human mold, with the human at its center, from the very start makes it impossible for things to speak as things. This brings us back to the beginning. Probably, when such personification or emotionalization is completely eliminated, at the limits of the gaze that sees things as things, they repel the gaze of the self and appear bathed in a true quality of fantasy. Fantasy that does not reach that point is little more than a sodden emotion that emerges from the jumbled confusion of this shore and the other shore, attesting merely to the frailty of the self's gaze. Fantasy and emotion are of course two sides of the same coin. The fantastic belongs to the realm of things that rise up to repel the gaze of the self. And yet, at the same time, emotion betrays looking and is born from mystifying one's interior. For example, the fantastic quality of the novels of Alain Robbe-Grillet or Le Clézio is unmistakably of the kind I have described. Alternatively, while clearly distinct from those two, doesn't the eroticism and fantastic quality that emerges in Mandiargues's excellent short story "Platonic Solids," which describes the minutest fragments of objects "objectively," speak of the thickness of the flesh of these things?[12] This is an eroticism born of the discovery of things as things, and of the fact that they continue to exist as things. Alain Robbe-Grillet has spoken about his careful method of writing novels, and the need to eliminate all forms of personification (for example, expressions like "squatting mountain range" or "fickle weather") together with their associated symbols and allegories. The critique of his novels as mere objective description is completely misplaced. That is because personification, and its method of using symbols and allegories, only explains the world made to the measure of the human. Is it even possible to explain the world? And if the world could be explained, would its explanation be necessary? Rather than explaining, Robbe-Grillet depicts "objectively"; through depiction (which is the stream of consciousness itself) he merely tries to make clear the absolute division that exists between things and the self. We gaze at things, and charge at them in order to possess them. But things offer nothing at all in response. Our gaze is simply repelled by the hard exterior of things. Things constantly withdraw in the face of our gaze. But precisely from this point—the point where the gaze of the self is repelled—it can be said that things start to cast their gaze back toward the self.

A site tinged with magnetic energy, where the gaze of the self is woven together with the gaze of things—that is the world. This discussion is hardly limited to the Nouveau Roman or similar kinds of novels.[13] The issue is that thinking in general, which for so long we have not doubted, must now itself be questioned.

In art and all other genres of expression, we are already developing expressive acts to bring forth such a "site." But how about our photography? What validity can photography have for such thinking? In any case, for me as a photographer, this is a raw and actual question.

Kōji Taki, my former magazine companion and still one of my closest friends, said of my photobook that the work emerges from "lending one's body to the world." Still, he also wrote that "a thing that exceeds the subject determines the subject," and he criticized my romantic frustration toward this.[14] At that time, when I drank, I would prattle on: "The world would still exist whether I'm here or not. But if I'm not here, whether or not the world exists is of no concern to me." Perhaps I am only now coming to grasp the meaning of all this. But if we pursue Taki's words to the end, they obviously go well beyond my photobook. Then again, if critique is something by which a critic narrates themselves through the medium of a single work, this may not deserve any special mention. But it is certain that my thinking has now arrived at the gaze of things that repels my gaze. Such a vaguely self-critical stance is excruciating, but in speaking a little more about the photographs I've taken to this point, and by clarifying their limitations, I am seized with the impulse to delineate the contours of a photography to come. Is it truly the case, as the critic I cited at the beginning of this essay has it, that I am trying to construct for my photographs "a poisoned meaning through a poisoned language"? And yet, I will dare to repeat this stupidity.

Looking back on my own photographs, I wonder why I focused almost exclusively on "night," "dusk," or "dawn." Why did I shoot only in monochrome, not color? Further, why did I prefer a rough grain, or intentional blurring? Was this no more than a question of technique? Of course, that may have been the case. But, at a deeper level, I think I can say it came from the relationship between myself and the world. To state the conclusion up front, I think this relationship made the space between myself and the subject ambiguous, to forcefully assert my possession of the world, my recreation of the world according to my own image. "Poetry" and emotion were born out of this ambiguity. This meant trying to use the mechanism of the camera for an old-fashioned kind of "expression," or "art." My landscapes that "suggest the end of the world" were, truly, an expression of my a priori image. And so, for that reason, I chose "night," when the world dissolves. Without a doubt, my choice of monochrome film complemented this, because monochrome film stubbornly retains some "trace of the hand" (darkroom work still involves a degree of handicraft). Rough grain and blur did not emerge as a method inevitably derived from the encounter between the self and the world, as in the case of William Klein. Instead, they were nothing more than a way to sneak in the personification of emotion, to fill in the blank that emerged when I abandoned the act of seeing before gazing at the world—before I could confirm that things were things themselves, in their nakedness. That there was "poetry" in my photos must itself be turned around and made into a criticism of my work. Things dissolving into "night" and "darkness"—doesn't that attest to the fact that I abandoned the act of seeing and, at the same time, to the fact that my eyes were closed to the gaze of things, at the very moment when things fulfill themselves as things? Of course, up until that point, all manner of photographs were ultimately no more than illustrations that reduced the meaning of the world to stereotyped schemas, and I had set out as a photographer seized with the almost reckless impulse to negate them. All the same, though, I fell into another trap. In the end, I myself degenerated into a subspecies of them.

Of course, I've been speaking in an extremely fragmented way about the self-expansion of things, about the gaze returned by things, and about a certain kind of fear toward things as things themselves. But these are no more than impulsive thoughts. If so, why didn't I choose "daylight"?

Let me quote from Le Clézio once more:

> The anxiety of daylight likely gives us more fear than the anxiety of night. This is not because we fall prey to an elusive enemy, but because here we confront unforgiving violence directly, the severity, the cruelty of life itself. Our fear comes not from some unknown existence that bores its way into an abyss, but from the violent rise of actual existence, from some kind of tangible vertigo that spreads out, exposing and eradicating us. That which is all too visible harbors a greater menace than that which cannot be seen.[15]

In daylight, things exist as they are, as things. They are naked, with line, form, and mass, and yet our gaze can only trace their surfaces. Without question, this is a source of anguish for us. We wish to give things a name, and thereby possess them. However, things reject this, and they become things through this rejection. Against the encroachment of the eye, things set up a defense—and now, they begin their encroachment toward us. Let us recognize the existence of things without adjectives (that is, without meaning), in eternity, things existing solely through the logic of things. Things exist like this, not some other way. Let us recognize this. There is no room for any poesy to intervene. Poesy or poetry only arises when I close my eyes to the antagonism of the absolute incompatibility of my gaze with the gaze of things. Then, my "feelings" blur the outline of things. Clearly, this is my own "presumption," and at the same time, my own "laziness of the eye." Already burdened with systematized meanings, all that the eye seeks from the world is to confirm these meanings. The eye is no longer a transparent window to the world, but instead transforms into a shelter that closes me off from the world. The world becomes a reverse projection of myself.

The existence of things under the brilliance of the midday sun. To wipe away all shadows from things. Let there be light! These shadows themselves are the last fortress of the "human."

3

What is a camera? On what logic does a camera depend? The camera could be called an embodiment of our desire to look; a technology borne of the historical accumulation of that desire; or a system in and of itself. The camera objectifies everything, making the world into an object by distancing it from the self. By cutting reality into a square frame, and reducing it to a single point, the self can possess this, even if it is only a fragment of reality. In that sense, the camera is inevitably saddled with the binary opposition between subject and object that is the foundational logic of modernity. However, looking cannot happen apart from the body. Nor is it possible to live as a body in the world without looking. In this way, the body passes through the world, and space either spreads through the body, or, perhaps, becomes corporealized; all of this composes a world, and its "memories." And all of this is the true state of seeing. The world is not simply an object produced through my own objectification. Does this contradict the thesis I have put forth until now, which affirms the absolute discordance between myself and things? Not in the slightest. That is because the world itself is the magnetic field in which my gaze, and the gaze of things thrown back at it, struggle against one another. To look is also to expose the self to the gaze of the other. But before making this into a schema, the self must first confirm that things are truly things as they are, and not possessions of the self. There is the world, and then there is the self.

However, as the product of modernity par excellence, the camera forces the world into single-point perspective. The camera unilaterally restricts the act of looking to the eye of the self. As a result, it embodies the thought that seeks to operate the world. If that is the case, then by its very nature isn't the camera a method incapable of grasping the world in total? Such a question is extremely natural to pose. Certainly, to the extent that one takes up a single photograph, it does no more than present the space into which the single point that is the self has unilaterally peered. But if one is not limited to the space of a single photograph, and considers instead the innumerable photographs mediated by time and place, doesn't the meaning of the perspective of each individual photograph gradually fade? In other words, it is possible that the mediation of time in this way, endlessly surpassing and being surpassed, might clarify the structure of the world as a place that encompasses the dualistic opposition of self and world. Wouldn't the static schema of self and world then disappear, to be replaced by the structuration of an endlessly moving and unlimited number of perspectives? Without a doubt, conditions would change a little if that were to take place successfully. If I continue to pursue photography, and, however little, bet on its potential, it would likely be for this reason. The year before last, I undertook this kind of expressive act with *Date, Place, Events*, an installation at a certain exhibition of art.[16] This installation showed the innumerable realities with which I came into contact on certain days, but it did not only show what I saw—at times, my own self was fixed on film, in "photographized" form. All this was displayed day after day. Of course, on account of the immaturity of my own thinking, and the poor physical conditions of the space, I was unable to make this thought clear, but looking back now, I was without a doubt motivated by what I have written above. The idea was to overcome the perspective of individual photographs by greatly multiplying their numbers. Even if I could not overcome these perspectives, I could at least move toward nullifying them. I think this is accurate enough as a loose description.

And yet, upon further reflection, this collapse of perspective is spreading widely at the level of the everyday life we must live out. If we limit ourselves to speaking individually about the overwhelming number of images that the mass media constantly broadcasts to us, we can say that each one is necessarily based on a single perspective; however, to speak from the full range of sensorial levels through which we receive them all at once, they have already made it impossible for the self to establish a perspective that could absorb them all into a single point. For example, all the fragmentary realities displayed on television (needless to say, though, they can only be pseudo-realities precisely because they are fragmentary) do nothing but confuse us. They are reedited and embedded into a reality with a single orientation; in other words, they strip away the very foundation of the process of making meaning. From news to home dramas, the cooking hour to sports, along with the intervention of short commercials that weave them all together—how, and through what perspective, could we possibly organize these images one by one, and give them order? Gōsuke Uchimura has aptly called those of us who now live in this kind of reality "consumers of history."[17]

I happen to have used television and the consciousness of the masses as they receive its broadcast images as an example, but this only reflects one minute aspect of the basic character of the dissolution of the individual, a process that dominates the contemporary moment. The contemporary city has become a giant monster that pulverizes us. One by one, the foundation of our identity as individuals is shaken by the city. Every day, we are continually steeped in an overflow of products, an overflow of information, and an overflow of things. Our "center" has been lost. The abnormal development of our technology has completely reversed the character of materials and information into which everything could once converge. Technology continues to proliferate itself, and as a result, we have lost any "center" that could correspond to the scattered profusion of such vast quantities of materials and information. The dissolution of the world corresponds precisely to the dissolution of this "center." One option would be to naively grieve this. But now that the situation has come this far, there is no way to reverse it. We might even turn it to our advantage. First, we must admit "the defeat of the human" and seek out a legitimate place, one free of privilege, for the existence of humans as humans in a world where things exist as things. Because we have never lived in a similar age, the question of whether this is the terrain of absolute nihilism or absolute freedom is, in a certain sense, impossible to pose. The protagonist of Godard's film *Weekend* is the vast amount of blood that flows from innumerable traffic accidents, while the two people who try to escape in any direction whatsoever are practically miniaturized beings, but the reason that we can feel the film with such rawness is because we truly live in such an age. The city overflows. Things overflow, and rebellion begins. The important thing is to desperately accept this. That is the point of departure.

However, how do we relate to what we are accustomed to calling art or expression? We have stuck to a received concept of art, and as far as we continue to adhere strictly to such traditional forms of expression, it is clear that we can do no more than individually lament the state of the world through expression or art. Still, the task of bringing forth and revealing the symptoms of the age remains to us. That is because, insofar as we can confirm with certainty that our image of the world as being in a certain way has collapsed, it is already clear that the work of art as a development and expression of an image belonging to an individual can do nothing at all. Further, sticking to such closed-off expression or work means disregarding the existence of the self in the world. Is it even possible to bring forth expression or work from a place that is detached from both reality and the self? Of course, the answer is obvious.

In "Toward a Reading of Forms," Jean Rousset cites the following passage written by Gaëtan Picon: "There is a modern consciousness about art which, compared to the consciousness that preceded it, suggests to us that an art of creation has come to supplant an art of expression. Before modern art, the work seemed to be the expression of an anterior experience . . . the work expressed what had been seen or thought; so much so that the passage from the experience to the work involved only a technique of execution. For modern art, the work is not an expression but a creation; it reveals what had not been seen before, it forms rather than reflects."[18]

"How could the work of art claim to illustrate a signification known in advance, whatever it might be? The modern novel, as we said at the start, is an exploration, but an exploration which itself creates its own significations, as it proceeds."[19] (Robbe-Grillet)

"The first thing we must do is abandon completely the concept of 'representation.' What can rescue art from the closed circuit of 'civilization' is pressure (*pression*) applied to art, not expression (*expression*). The world will absolutely not be changed by people expressing their 'selves.'"[20] (Alain Jouffroy)

I am citing at random, but the point is that our temporal axis that establishes an individual as an individual is already in tatters. It is impossible for us to summarize the world into a story (this does not refer strictly to literature). The world truly strikes us in its bare form, as so many dismantled fragments.

Beginning with literature and fine art, the form of every genre is being reexamined today through various means. But ultimately, this begins with a reexamination of the relation between the self and the modern world and is an effort *to confirm the human, and the position of the human in the world*—a point that needs no further explanation. To offer just a few examples, Nouveau Roman writers diligently use the word *text* instead of *work*, while contemporary artists reject works that circulate in favor of actions. In the sense that they express an already confirmed meaning of the world, they do not set out to express anything at all. Still, through their actions, they strive to show things and the self, and the structure of the world in which these two struggle with each other. More often than not, these efforts take an overly hasty form, or an extreme form that renders them incomplete or undercooked. But it would clearly be a mistake to laugh this all off, because at the very foundation of their understanding is the proposition that the world is incomplete, and that the self is also incomplete. In a certain sense, then, it is all too natural for their expression to be incomplete. Being incomplete is synonymous with being open.

Why an illustrated botanical guide? To this point, in taking the form of a roundabout and chaotic response to the critical letter that was addressed to me, I believe I have accounted for why I am no longer able to take pictures as before; why I am sick of such photography; and, although this was actually subconscious, why "poetry" has fallen out of my photographs. I have written all this as a response to the reader's letter, but it is of course also a way for me to confirm something for myself: that, in sum, our expression in this age must discard the image, face up to the world as it is, and properly arrange things in the world, with things as things, and the self as the self. For this purpose, the anthropomorphization and emotionalization of the world by the self must first be rejected. Beyond this, no more general or abstract discourse is needed. The next, and more concrete questions must be: What should I do, and is it possible to do it through the method of photography?

Although it is vague to me now, there is work pressing on me with the force of an obsession, and I would like to start on it as quickly as possible.[21] For some reason, I am calling it an "illustrated botanical guide."[22] Plants, illustrated guides, and the connections between these two words are strangely compelling to me. Why plants? Why an illustrated guide? There is no way

I could completely account for everything, and I am afraid that talking about this now might dissolve the work before it has even started. Having come this far, though, I cannot avoid offering an outline given its connection with what I have written up until this point. I have already published photographs with the title *Illustrated Botanical Guide* in a certain magazine.[23] This was almost certainly the catalyst for the illustrated botanical guide to expand within me.

Above all else, it is an illustrated guide, the sort of book that is often for children: an illustrated guide to fish, an illustrated guide to alpine plants, an illustrated guide to colored carp, and so on. The most important function of an illustrated guide is to display its given objects clearly and directly. An illustrated guide rejects all shading, and any emotion that might steal in. There is no such thing as an illustrated guide to "sad-looking" cats. If an illustrated guide has even the slightest trace of ambiguity, it no longer fulfills its function as an illustrated guide. Illustrated guides are characterized by enumeration and juxtaposition. They are not totalities assembled around some central, privileged thing. In other words, the parts that are there *are not parts absorbed into a totality*; these parts always remain parts, and there is nothing beyond them. The method of the illustrated guide is one of strict juxtaposition.[24] This method of juxtaposition, in turn, must itself become my own method. Also, the illustrated guide does no more than adhere closely to the sparkling surface of things. It strictly refuses my own vulgar curiosity, my pretension to search for meaning beyond or within things; it only establishes itself by clarifying that things are things. This must, in turn, become my own method.

Out of necessity, then, an illustrated guide fundamentally rejects poesy, "darkness," or "dusk." That is why illustrated guides somewhat resemble catalogs. Catalogs also eliminate any and all ambiguity; they merely display commodities directly. If a commodity is not shown in minute detail, the catalog no longer fulfills its function. The idea of an ambiguous catalog is itself a logical contradiction.

So, why plants? Why an illustrated botanical guide and not an illustrated animal guide, or an illustrated mineral guide? Animals stink too much of life, while from the very beginning minerals flaunt the robust qualities of the other shore. What lies between them are plants. In their veins, sap, etc., there still remains something that resembles our own flesh. In other words, they are organic bodies. From an intermediary position, they leap impulsively and sink into me—such are plants. Plants still retain some sort of vagueness. To grasp the vagueness of plants means just barely marking out the boundary between plants and myself. That is the illustrated botanical guide I am secretly planning. In Le Clézio's *The Interrogation*, which I mentioned above, the protagonist Adam Pollo goes swimming at the beach with a female friend on a summer day. As the sun bakes his back over a long period of time, Adam remains silent. The female friend casually calls out to him. His long silence interrupted, Adam breaks into a sudden anger, saying that he was just on the cusp of entering the mineral stage, and that without a doubt, he had already entered the plant stage. Just what is this? To turn oneself into a single world, into a stone object. To turn oneself into a single thing, lined up alongside stones, leaves, waves, and all kinds of other things. This is, in the end, impossible, because the self is afflicted by the devilish disease called consciousness. And yet, to be conscious is not to be the ruler of the world, as has been believed. To be conscious is to be conscious of the self as an other. This is also a reflection of being conscious of the other, and conscious of things.

In any case, I think I will begin my work once more through the illustrated botanical guide. I will capture things in broad daylight, using color photography, and put them into an illustrated botanical guide. No matter what, these photographs must be in color. That is because, as I have already written, I think I need to rid myself once and for all of the "traces of the hand" that are present in black-and-white darkroom work. That hand itself is the thing that has established art. The hand—an other within the self. But at the same time the hand is, after all, the self. And that which is manipulated by the hand is, after all, an extension of the hand. The world is manipulated by the hand. My illustrated botanical guide begins where this world breaks off. In that sense, color photography is already of the other shore.

Once the shutter is clicked, everything ends.

First published in *Why an Illustrated Botanical Guide? Collected Writings on Images by Takuma Nakahira* (Shōbunsha, 1973).

Notes

1 "The Illusion Called Document: From Document to Monument," which appears in this volume (see page 36), was first published in the art magazine *Bijutsu Techō*, July 1972, 73–87.

2 In this essay, when Nakahira uses the word *image* on its own, he is referring to the Japanese word *imēji*, which points to an abstracted idea of the image, perhaps closer to *imagination*, rather than to specific images produced by specific technologies.

3 Here, the letter writer cites Nakahira's essay "The Return of Reality," *Design*, January 1969, 56.

4 This citation is from "The Illusion Called Document."

5 Tomō Yoshikawa, "To Takuma Nakahira," *Bijutsu Techō*, August/September 1972, 228–29.

6 Here, Nakahira is referring to *For a Language to Come* (1970).

7 Alain Robbe-Grillet, *For a New Novel*, trans. Richard Howard (New York: Grove Press, 1965), 19.

8 Although Nakahira does not cite any text here, this may be a reference to the writings of the contemporary artist Lee Ufan, whose book *In Search of Encounter* (1971) Nakahira designed.

9 Jean-Marie Gustave Le Clézio, *Le Procès-Verbal* (*The Interrogation*, Paris: Gallimard, 1963). Nakahira is quoting from Kōichi Toyosaki's 1966 translation.

10 Nakahira used the phrase "impermeable crust" in a short text he wrote to accompany his photographs, under the title "Illustrated Botanical Guide," in the news magazine *Asahi Journal*, August 20, 1971.

11 Eugène Guillevic, "Les Murs," trans. John Montague, in Harry Gilonis, ed., *Dubuffet's Walls: Lithographs for "Les Murs"* (London: Hayward Gallery Publishing, 1999).

12 The story that Nakahira refers to by French writer André Pieyre de Mandiargues (1909–1991) has not been translated into English. In French, see André Pieyre de Mandiargues, “Les corps platoniciens,” in *Marbre* (Paris: Robert Laffont, 1953), 55–91. A Japanese translation of this collection by Tatsuhiko Shibusawa and Takako Takahashi was published in 1971.

13 The term Nouveau Roman, or New Novel in English, refers to an experimental mode of literature that emerged in France during the 1950s. Robbe-Grillet and Le Clézio are among its representative writers.

14 Nakahira quotes a review that Taki published of *For a Language to Come* in *Design*, December 1970, 18.

15 Jean-Marie Gustave Le Clézio, *L'Extase matérielle* (Paris: Gallimard, 1967). Nakahira does not provide a page number; he cites the 1971 translation of Le Clézio's book into Japanese by Kōichi Toyosaki.

16 This is the installation, *Circulation: Date, Place, Events*, that Nakahira presented at the 1971 Paris Biennale, held from September 24 to November 1 at the Parc Floral de Paris. Nakahira also refers to this exhibition in “Why Jazz Now? Preface to a Theory of Place”; see page 62 in this volume.

17 Gōsuke Uchimura (1920–2009) was a writer and critic who specialized in Russian literature. The phrase that Nakahira quotes appears in his essay “‘History’ Is Nothing More than a Product: Images in the Age of the Loss of Perspective,” which was published in *Bijutsu Techō*, June 1972, 38–56.

18 Jean Rousset, “Toward a Reading of Forms,” trans. David Gorman, *Style* 29, no. 1 (1995): 132–48. This text was published in Rousset's essay collection *Forme et signification: essai sur les structures littéraires de Corneille à Claudel* (Paris: José Corti, 1964).

19 Robbe-Grillet, *For a New Novel*, 141.

20 Nakahira quotes the Japanese translation of Jouffroy's essay “The Abolition of Art,” which has not been translated into English at the time of writing. In this Japanese translation, the French terms *pression* and *expression* were rendered in parentheses. See Alain Jouffroy, “The Abolition of Art,” trans. Toshiaki Minemura, *Design Hihyō*, no. 8 (January 1969): 11–25.

21 In this paragraph, and for the remainder of the essay, the word that Nakahira uses for *work*, *shigoto*, carries no connotations of art, unlike the word *sakuhin*, also translated as *work* but which is used in the case of art and literature. *Shigoto* is more appropriate to *work* in the sense of a job, not artistic creation.

22 Among existing references to the present essay in English-language scholarship, the word *zukan* has usually been translated as either

"illustrated encyclopedia" or "illustrated dictionary." We have chosen instead to render it as "illustrated guide." In English, the words *encyclopedia* and *dictionary* describe books with highly specialized and limited functions, both of which are text-driven. In Japanese, *zukan* designates a much wider range of books that introduce subjects in various registers—but which are, by definition, structured by visual illustrations. For example, the well-known series of field guides published in the United States by the National Audubon Society would certainly be considered *zukan*. However, as Nakahira points out, the term also encompasses pictorial guides for children, which can be quite short, and deal with one specific topic only: "an illustrated guide to fish, an illustrated guide to alpine plants, an illustrated guide to colored carp, and so on." In fact, Nakahira uses the word *zukan* again in the essay "Interlude," collected in this volume, when he describes "the figure of a large snapping shrimp, with one enlarged claw, that I had seen in one of my child's illustrated guides"; see page 145.

23 Nakahira published photographs under this title in the weekly news magazine *Asahi Journal* (August 20, 1971). A series with this title later appeared in the July 1973 issue of the Japanese magazine *Design*.

24 The word *juxtaposition* appears in English in the original. In the following sentence, Nakahira then uses the Japanese word *heichi*.

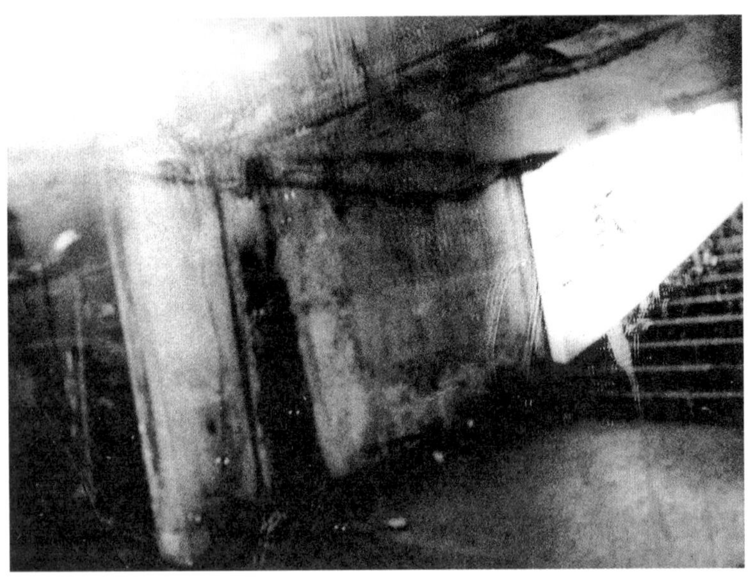

Takuma Nakahira, *Untitled*, from the photobook *For a Language to Come*, 1970

Eugène Atget: The Look Toward the City, or the Look from the City

It is already irreversible. Whenever I am presented with the photographs of Eugène Atget, I am overcome with this feeling. For a very long time, I have tried to figure out just where it comes from. This is also the main reason why I am attracted to Atget. Yet, now that I must write about Atget once more, it will not do to simply describe such vague impressions.

Eugène Atget: an artisan of photography, who took photographs of the streets of fin-de-siècle Paris in the grips of destitution, eked out a living by selling them as "documents for artists," and died alone in obscurity and poverty. But there is also the Atget who, after his death, was a tremendous influence on the Surrealist movement. This has even become a kind of myth. Starting with Berenice Abbott, many people have described the humanistic aspects of Atget, and this story will be handed down for generations to come. But with my highly personal feelings of attraction to Atget as my only lead, I will instead think about Eugène Atget, and further, about just what photography is.

The "irreversible" sensation I feel when looking at Atget's photographs may certainly arise from the spatial and temporal gap between fin-de-siècle Paris and myself in the present. But if that was all, then we already know of so many other photographs that have this kind of nostalgia, or that cause us to yearn for far-off places. The sole value of these photographs, of which there are many, is to transport ever older, ever more distant things to us in the present.

Unlike these, each one of Atget's photographs goes beyond this enormous gap of space and time, and while I am entangled with the distant memories of experiences I encountered and landscapes I saw somewhere during my not-so-short life, I am brutally confronted with the "irreversible" thought that I have absolutely never existed before *this* specific landscape, this street that Atget captured. Or, perhaps it is better to say instead that Atget's is the kind of photography where, in the end, these streets and things thoroughly repel me. I am using the word "irreversible" to convey this. Certainly, I have seen this sort of sculpture in a park somewhere, and seen the sculpture and trees reflected in the surface of a pond in the same way. Certainly, I have felt midsummer rays of sunlight pour upon me, filtering through the trees just like this. I have a childhood memory of drifting through antiquated street corners like these, with those walls full of *stains*. But even so, *this* sunlight of Atget's that filters through the trees, this street corner of Atget's—they are absolutely not my own.

In the end, Atget's images [*eizō*] reject my own memories and feelings; the streets coldly stare back at me as streets, and the things stare back at me as things.[1] There is no space in them for my own meaning or sentimentalization to seep in. They entwine themselves with my memories, and yet ultimately, they reject them completely, with a kind of twist. Atget's photographs hang suspended in midair, between such catharsis and a feeling of rejection mixed with estrangement. This is probably the main feature of Atget's photography.

All the same, there are no human figures in Atget's photographs. As Walter Benjamin has aptly pointed out, they call to mind "crime scenes."[2] Even when people appear in them, their personalities have been scraped off, and most have somehow been completely embedded within the city, or within things. Streets, people, and things are all equal here, having been stripped of their shadows and fallen into complete silence. They jolt one awake, like catching a glimpse of the world through the pale fluorescent light beyond the glass fish tanks lined up in an aquarium. And this strikes fear into the viewer.

However, just what does it mean to see? Of course, I understand that to see is to possess and give meaning to the world by establishing a secure distance between myself and the subject, reducing the world to a *thing* (a subject) that must be visible. But what happens if this distance breaks down? This is a bit personal, but a few years ago I was hospitalized for close to a month with symptoms of constant perceptual irregularity that were brought about as a result of my habitual use of sleeping pills, which I had been taking for insomnia. It is difficult to briefly describe the hallucinations I had at the time. I call them hallucinations, yet it was not that I was having visions of something that was not there. This condition was instead the breakdown of this sense of distance, a loss of the balance that ought to have existed between things and me.

For example, if I was at a café talking with a friend, I would suddenly notice a glass on the table. But in that instant, I could not tell the distance between the glass and myself. As a result, I was unable to recognize the glass as a glass. When seized by such an attack, it was like I was paralyzed with fear, and although at the time I completely lost the ability to calmly analyze what was happening, I would look back later and realize that this was exactly the case.

Looking out at the scenery through a train window, things would suddenly come toward me and pierce my eyeballs. In order to protect myself in the speeding railcar (so strong was the anxiety that I would be unable to control myself and leap out the window) I had to close my eyes and tightly clutch the armrest. As this perceptual irregularity got worse, seeing things became a matter of things directly piercing my eyeballs, and I came to firmly believe that consciousness was the scar tissue from these wounds that things inflicted directly upon my eyeballs, or upon my retina. Unable to walk the streets, I was hospitalized. It's not as though this anxiety has been completely eliminated, for even now my consciousness is taken over by that of a sick person. Isn't "to see" just the inverse of the expression that "things come stabbing toward me"? I know this is all very abrupt, but just now I suddenly recalled all of this while looking at Atget's photobook *Paris du temps perdu*.

I have been casually describing "the photographs of Eugène Atget." But perhaps it would be more appropriate to say, "the worlds that accidentally entered the camera operated by the professional artisan of photography named Eugène Atget." In other words, Atget did not take photographs according to a predetermined image of his own. He turned the camera toward the street corners of Paris, and to things of all kinds. These, in turn, were imprinted onto dry plates in accordance with the laws of optics. We cannot ignore the conditions of film and camera development at this time, as they decisively shaped the characteristics of his photographs. Low-sensitivity film required long exposure times, which completely removed the forms of people walking by on the street. This also made it impossible to take photographs at night. So, these photographs that resemble "crime scenes" were in no way the realization or the externalization of predetermined images that he had in mind. On the contrary, they became that way out of necessity. It is an undeniable fact that the level of technological advancement in photography of that era decided the nature of Atget's images. In this sense, too, his photographs were not photographs permeated by his own consciousness. Instead, it was the elements that Atget was not conscious of, the elements of the unconscious, which decided the nature of his photographs. Even today, we are moved when we see Atget's photographs precisely because, through his camera, the world ruled by this "unconscious" can still shake our consciousness. Walter Benjamin precisely grasps something like this in his "Little History of Photography":

> No matter how artful the photographer, no matter how carefully posed his subject, the beholder feels an

> irresistible urge to search such a picture for the tiny spark of contingency, of the here and now, with which reality has (so to speak) seared the subject, to find the inconspicuous spot where in the immediacy of that long-forgotten moment the future nests so eloquently that we, looking back, may rediscover it. *For it is another nature which speaks to the camera rather than to the eye: "other" above all in the sense that a space informed by human consciousness gives way to a space informed by the unconscious.*[3]

Of course, it is obvious that the "nature" spoken of here does not refer to trees and plants. In Atget's case, "nature" could be swapped out for "the city," or "things." I wrote before that I feel that I cannot enter into Atget's photographs. I think this is closely related to the fact that Atget discarded predetermined images and took photographs as an artisan, thereby drawing us into a world beyond any imposed "meaning," where we feel disoriented under the naked, hostile gaze of things. Such an operation of estrangement, or estrangement effect, is what resulted in Atget's influence on the Surrealists; said in reverse, it is what drew the Surrealist artists to Atget's photographs.

If we consider that what gave rise to Surrealism as a movement was an era that had begun to fundamentally question all values in the wake of the collapse of the preestablished harmony of the world following World War I, we can fully comprehend the fact that in order to reexamine the world and their own position in it, young artists set out to return things to the world of things, and to question piece by piece the entire system of meanings, values, and images that had been historically constructed up until that point in time. This was also an effort to rescue the human, to locate a rightful position for the human in the world by pushing things back to the side of things. Considered in this way, we can understand why the Surrealists started to pay attention to Eugène Atget's photographs. The fantastical atmosphere and surreal feeling that pervade Atget's images emerge from the naked things that peek out from fissures in humanistic meaning.

However, photographers since Eugène Atget, photographers as so-called "authors" of modernity, have gone off in a completely different direction from him. As history bears out, they have instead clung to their predetermined, personal images, and tried to remake the world in line with such images, in order to establish their individual selves as "artists." To cite a few examples at random, this is probably true of the abstractionist Alvin Langdon Coburn, the photogram artist László Moholy-Nagy, Albert Renger-Patzsch of the *Neue Sachlichkeit*, and Edward Weston of Group f/64.

Moholy-Nagy, Renger-Patzsch, and Weston have certainly worked to broaden our vision, by first turning their eyes to minuscule parts of reality and things, and then presenting them in expanded ways. Ultimately, though, this only culminated in another new aesthetic—one in which reality became tangled up with images. Furthermore, it seems to me that the so-called straight photography of photojournalists and reportage photographers like Alfred Stieglitz, Edward Steichen, and Dorothea Lange seeks out the meaning of "poverty" or "suffering" from reality, only to extract and display nothing more than these literal meanings. Of course, this is putting it a bit strongly. There must be a more suitable commentator on these histories than me. But if I might dare to speak from my own biases, among the century-long history of photography, I think the only person comparable to Eugène Atget is Walker Evans, who photographed the impoverishment of American rural areas following the Great Depression of 1929.

So just who, exactly, is the photographer? As a photographer myself, whenever I think about Eugène Atget I am always left with this question. This also raises the question: Does the photographer as "author" exist? Of course, photographers do exist today as vocational specialists, and I am a petty ranking member among them. Yet, if we consider that the "author" is someone who "produces" the world by literally asserting the "self," then there is no need for the photographer as "author" to exist. This should be clear from what I have already written on Atget thus far. Because he did not have a predetermined image, Atget succeeded in ushering in the world, ushering in reality. Because he lacked any such image, Atget laid bare the world as the world. But is that possible for us, who already know too much whether we like it or not? If it were to be possible, the only way to start would be to discard one's self.

Ben Vautier, a French contemporary artist who tirelessly writes out slogans, has said: "If you want to change the world, to change art, first lose your ego."[4] It is just as he says. The photographer can no longer obtain anything by asserting the individual self. By doing so, one might at best succeed in adding one's name to the continuously drifting course of photographic history as a photographer of the system, as an artist of the system—nothing more. This means enclosing oneself in a system, as an officially sanctioned "holy artist." In a lecture titled "Literature as a System," Hans Magnus Enzensberger notes that until the era of Guy de Maupassant, literature possessed a certain normative social capacity—the power to influence a shared sense of material values, aesthetics, morals—but that from the twentieth century on, with the growth of productive capacities that brought forth a variety of mass media like photography, radio, and television, literature lost the power to regulate the consciousness (and the subconscious) of the masses. For Enzensberger, the literature that can still endure today will become a "literature among the catacombs," in other words the prized possession of an extremely limited and privileged few. This points directly to the state of photography, and the photographer, from now on.

Photography "as art"—this will be placed in the hands of a privileged few. And, at the same time, as this sort of art photography becomes increasingly divorced from reality and history, it will become that much more "holy." However, it will not attain photography's intrinsic potentiality, which is to expand our perception, and to lay the world bare (just as Atget's photographs do). On the contrary, with the development of film and photographic technologies, the masses will certainly come to hold the intrinsic function of photography more firmly in their hands. I said, "the masses." But that does not refer to "amateurs," those clumsy imitators of "authors." "Amateurs" are a colossal reserve army of future "authors." In a malignant way, they merely amplify and reproduce the aesthetics and images that "authors" brandish. The masses I refer to are, precisely, the anonymous masses. When photography is evaluated only on the basis of its intrinsic specificity—in other words, on the basis of how much it reveals the world, not who took the photograph—then it will obtain its true anonymity. The anonymity I speak of can only be achieved from within such a flow of history.

The discontinuation of *Life* magazine. This shows one aspect of the fact that photography has been surpassed by television and other more developed media. But to be more precise, we could say that *Life*'s way of treating photographs, where a reporter unilaterally conveys "true reality" to the masses as their spokesperson, has broken down as a form of communication for photography. In a more centralized and monopolistic form, television has taken this over. This may suggest that photography has, potentially, drawn closer to the side of the masses.

From this point on, will photography split off into two poles: the photography of "the photographer among the catacombs," and the photography of the masses? The photography of the masses will surely resemble Eugène Atget's photography. This will not be a photography measured by how much a single individual was able to capture the world with their personal image, but one measured by how much of the world is condensed in its true form on film in an instant. That kind of photography will manifest the intrinsic function of photography all the more vividly on the dimension called "society."

The first chapter of Eugène Atget's photobook *Paris du temps perdu* is titled "The Look Toward the City." But now, this must be restated as "The Look from the City." That is because these are not images of the city, images of the world grasped through a firmly established ego's gaze on the world, but instead a group of photographs that have, strangely, succeeded in inscribing the world and the city as they leap in from the other side, with what might be called a vacuum or concave eye.

In this sense, for us photographers, Eugène Atget persistently continues to ask us to return to the starting point, and reconsider: what is photography, and who is the photographer?

First published in the photography magazine *Asahi Camera*, November 1973. Later collected in *Duel on Photography* (coauthored with Kishin Shinoyama, Asahi Shimbunsha, 1977).

Notes

1 The word that Nakahira uses for *image*, *eizō*, refers specifically to an image that is produced through technical means, meaning that it could refer not just to photographs but also to cinema or television.

2 Here, Nakahira refers to Benjamin's essay "Little History of Photography," cited later in the essay. Although this description of Atget's photographs is often attributed to Benjamin, he is indirectly quoting other commentators from the 1920s.

3 Walter Benjamin, "Little History of Photography" in *Walter Benjamin: Selected Writings, vol. 2, 1927–1934* (Cambridge, Mass.: Belknap Press of Harvard University Press, 2001), 510. Emphasis is Nakahira's.

4 Nakahira is likely citing a work by Vautier (1935–2024), an artist associated with the Fluxus movement. In English, Vautier is known for his slogan "To change art destroy ego."

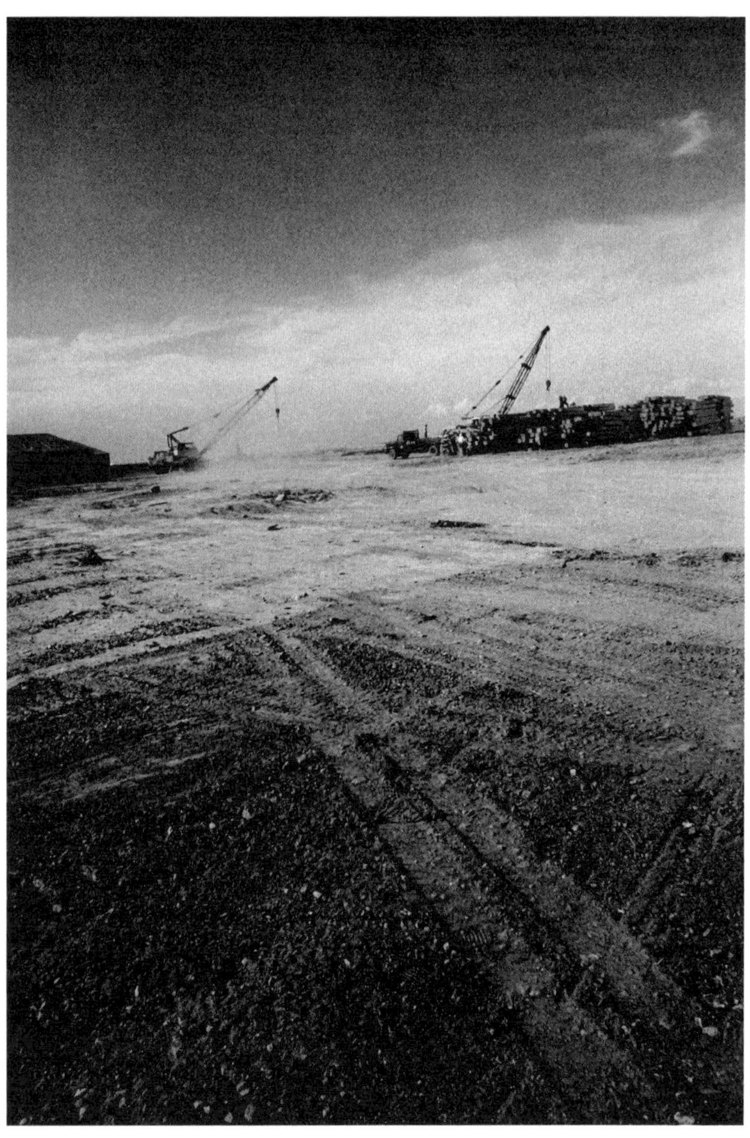

Takuma Nakahira, *Untitled*, from the photobook *For a Language to Come*, 1970

My Naked-Eye Reflex: 1974, Okinawa, Summer

Sunset on the East China Sea. To my right, Ie Island looks like a giant submarine. Cumulonimbus clouds burst into flames on the horizon. They rise, rise even further, and at their very top, merge into one enormous thundercloud. Each individual detail is entirely too vivid, and this overflowing energy directly strikes my eyeballs. Underneath the thundercloud must be Miyako Island, the Yaeyama Islands, and further along, Taiwan. Uotsuridai ought to be somewhere far out in front of me.[1]

Of course, the silhouettes of these islands cannot be seen from here. There is only the horizon, drawing a perfect horizontal line. Everything here is too clearly divided. Illuminated by the after-glow, a jet moves along soundlessly, leaving a straight contrail behind it. Everything is visible. The demolition of the coast here wrought by the construction of the Ocean Expo, and the firmly entrenched US-Japanese military bases: these also exist in plain sight, with no room for doubt.

At this moment, the main island of Okinawa is being continuously violated, through construction for the 1975 International Ocean Exposition centered on the Motobu area and its western coast; through the construction by Mitsubishi and other Japanese monopoly capital of a CTS (Central Terminal Station—a crude oil storage facility) in Kin Bay to the east; and through the gigantic US military bases in the center of the island that squeeze it like a pincer. Under the slogan "The Sea We Would Like to See," the Okinawa International Ocean Exposition is set to open in July 1975. This event has been planned to commemorate the 1972 "reversion" of Okinawa, but it was only made possible at first through the destruction of Okinawa's ocean and nature, and the sweeping destruction of the lives of the people who live on the island.[2]

About two years ago, I started to visit Okinawa with some frequency because of a certain frame-up trial.[3] The fact of the matter is that without this prompt, I think I certainly would not have gone to Okinawa. That is because I could not shake the premonition that to encounter Okinawa would shake the foundation of my existence at its root. And as I sit here now, I have many close friends in Okinawa. Still, I feel a certain distress when I talk about Okinawa. But I have to accept this and set off from there.

Just a year ago, the coast of the East China Sea leading to Motobu, the location of the Ocean Expo, was surrounded by coral reefs in the deep blue sea. Now, though, it has been transformed into a deep red sea of mud. Sediment that rushes down from the scraped-off surfaces of mountainsides is killing the sea. In its place, asphalt roads are steadily being laid down. There was a time when it seemed like the 1975 Ocean Expo might be cancelled or postponed, but now it looks like the majority of the construction has already been completed. This in exchange for the destruction of nature, and the destruction of the lives of the people who live there.

In reality, as a pamphlet titled *Okinawan Development and Regional Autonomy: The Problems of the Ocean Expo, Land Reclamation and the CTS* published by the Okinawa Prefectural and Municipal Workers Union aptly points out, the ocean of Okinawa has been destroyed and turned into a sea of mud, to the point that it is now "The Sea We Can't Bear to See." However, the important point is that the destruction of nature and the destruction of human life are proceeding on parallel tracks. The piercing logic behind this two-sided destruction is that anything can be sacrificed for the sake of profit. This is the logic of Mitsui, Fuyo, and Itochu, companies that pushed for the opening of the Ocean Expo, and the logic of Japanese imperialism that wanted to use the Expo as a lever for integrating Okinawa into the "New National Comprehensive Development Plan."

Not just Okinawa's main island, but also outlying islands such as Kerama, Miyako, and the Yaeyamas have all been incorporated into the process of making Okinawa into one enormous resort. The purchase of land through monopoly capital from the "mainland" has inevitably brought about the impoverishment of Okinawa's primary industries of farming and fishing. As a result, many people are forced into becoming half-farmers and half-professionals, or into leaving for the "mainland" as migrant workers. Moreover, the advance of mainland capital leaves two choices for small and medium-sized local enterprises: go bankrupt, or be swallowed up by "mainland" capital as subcontractors. The large investment from the "mainland," and the decline of the dollar just at the moment of "reversion" have caused unusually severe inflation. The seriousness of the situation is made clear by the abnormal monthly inflation rate of 18 percent. Clearly, the Ocean Expo is the main factor here.

In the truest sense of the term, the lives of Okinawan people are reaching a critical phase. Everything in that regard is visible. Just go into any restaurant on Kokusai-dori Street, in Naha. Just drive down the road that leads to Motobu. Just look at the CTS construction site in Kin Bay, and at the quagmire around it. Or just look at the US military bases that occupy the center of Okinawa, and at the repeated touch-and-go landings by the Self-Defense Forces at Naha Airport. The impoverishment and dismantling of Okinawa, the collapse of the lives of Okinawan people—all this can be seen with one's own eyes, with no room for ambiguity. Okinawan people call the "reversion" of May 15, 1972, the "third Ryūkyū disposition."[4] Yet even if we *yamantonchū*, we Japanese, were compelled to borrow this term, the "third Ryūkyū disposition" would not end.[5] At this moment, it is becoming reality.

What are Okinawan people thinking in the face of such destruction, and such visible crisis? Why hasn't a counteroffensive of Okinawan citizens burst forth? Yet, I know all too well that such questions are the questions of a bystander. We are just imposing our stereotyped thoughts onto Okinawan people. This is a common feature of both Japanese monopoly capital and the so-called "Japanese left wing." It's a cruel paradox. The impertinent questions we put forth are absorbed into the center of Okinawa, and no one can say where they go.

In Naha, slightly off the way from Heiwa-dori Street to Yogi, there is a farmer's market that is called "the stomach of Okinawa." In the early morning, before the sun rises, people start to work. They line up things like bitter melons, eggplants, cucumbers, and winter melons on the bare ground. Old people sell their things without uttering a word. What does the silence of those men and women say? Or what of the silence of the old women who sit in *uganju* (holy places)? Our questions are swallowed by their silence, left to wander aimlessly in space. However, when these men and women start to speak, won't that be the time when Okinawa will have its own language as Okinawa?

Now, in the predawn sky, cumulonimbus clouds are quietly billowing up, foretelling the intense heat to come. After wandering around Naha for an entire night, with exhausted limbs and a sleepless mind, such things come to my thoughts. Okinawa—"mainland." 1974, summer. Never mind my single-lens reflex—what will my naked-eye reflex actually have captured of Okinawa?

First published in the literary review newspaper *Nihon Dokusho Shimbun*, September 9, 1974.

Notes

1 Nakahira uses the Taiwanese name Uotsuridai to refer to an uninhabited island that is part of a group of islands called Senkaku in Japanese and Diaoyu in Chinese. These islands are the subject of a long-running territorial dispute between the governments of China and Japan.

2 Following the end of World War II, Okinawa was governed by the United States until May 15, 1972, when it was handed over to the Japanese government under a Reversion Agreement that maintained a significant US military presence.

3 Nakahira is referring to the trial of Yū Matsunaga; for more information, see the essay in this volume, "The Illusion Called Document: From Document to Monument," page 36.

4 "Disposition" (*shobun*) refers to historical moments of mainland Japanese incursion into Okinawa. The first disposition took place in 1609, when the Satsuma domain (present-day Kagoshima) invaded the Ryūkyū Kingdom; from that point it was under the dual subjugation of Satsuma and the Ming emperor. The second disposition occurred in 1879, when the Meiji state annexed the Ryūkyū Kingdom by force, and established Okinawa Prefecture.

5 Nakahira uses the Ryūkyūan word *yamantonchū* to describe mainland Japanese people, in order to mark the difference between these groups.

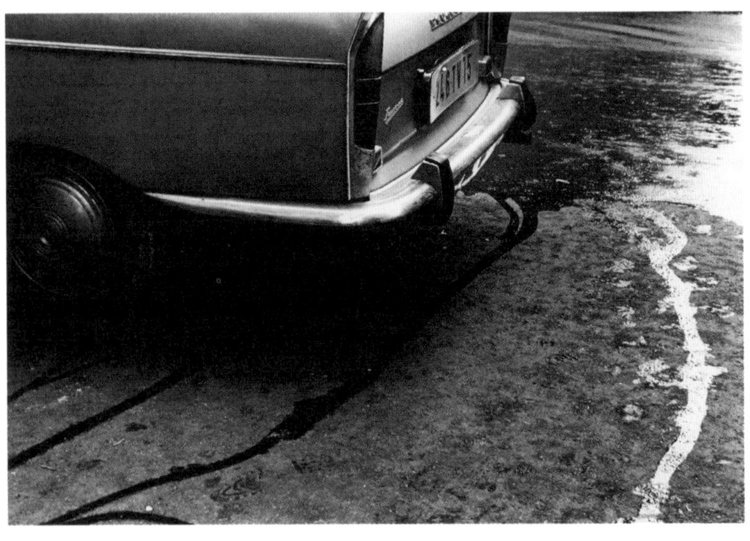

Takuma Nakahira, *Untitled*, from the series *Circulation: Date, Place, Events*, 1971

Things Crouched in Silence: On Walker Evans

I think it is already close to ten years since I first came in contact with Walker Evans's photographs. At that time, I was looking up materials related to Moholy-Nagy and the Bauhaus in a library in the center of Tokyo, while translating a book by György Kepes. Today, I am not even sure of that book's title. After finishing about three-quarters of the translation, I got dead drunk and lost both the original text and my draft, thanks to which I not only quit the publication of that book, but also broke off my work as a translator altogether.

One day while translating Kepes, I killed some time by taking a book off the shelf next to where I sat. Perhaps this was because my eyes were drawn to its strange title, *Let Us Now Praise Famous Men*. This relatively thick book scrupulously documented America's Great Depression of 1929, and the instability that continued into the 1930s—in particular, the "misery" that befell sharecroppers of America's Midwestern agricultural region and their families. The text was written by James Agee.

At that time, though, what drew my attention was not the text. It was not particularly fresh, and it did not leave any sort of strong impression. Though they take the form of a story or a drama, various John Steinbeck novels already describe the lives of people of the same period, existing under the same conditions, with brutal frankness. Also, while they have been received in Japan as popular fiction, novels of Erskine Caldwell such as *God's Little Acre* and *Tobacco Road* have also succeeded at laying bare the desires and tragedies of individual people in poor White families, in a sensational way that brings out a realistic depiction of their situations. Instead, what strongly attracted me at that time were the various photographs inserted in this text as illustrations.

I cannot recall all of them. But even now, I remember some quite clearly. A family all assembled on the dirt floor of a creaky farmhouse, doing their best, precisely because of their shabby clothes, to sit up straight for the photograph; a grave mound, utterly silent beneath the midday sun, with a single dish set on top of it; and finally, on the dirt wall of an abandoned house, a commemorative photograph of its former occupants, still tacked up, whose four corners had almost worn off. *A photograph of a photograph.* These photographs do not insist forcefully on anything: just like the pinned-up photograph that was left behind, they merely remain there as traces of the past. I thought that these photographs and the *photographs in the photographs* became mute because they were trying to speak of countless things—or rather, that they had no choice but to become mute, speaking only of the bottomless silence of the young girl, and that silence alone.

It was only after I became a photographer myself, thought about photography, and held forth about photographs that I learned these were the photographs of Walker Evans.

However, even when I think about Walker Evans and his photographs today, the double structure of the image found in these *photographs of photographs* always haunts me. At such a time, I have the feeling that I have perhaps managed to feel the specificity that only photographs possess, a silence at the limit of chatter—to say it the other way around, a way of photography that can transpose and fix a thing that cannot stop wishing to become "linguified" in the true sense of the word. When I think about photographs, I always feel myself returning to what I could call my own personal Walker Evans experience.

Walker Evans's photographs certainly do not speak of much. They crouch in silence. The things that Evans captures are not grandiose objects that could repel our gaze. There is no such aesthetic opacity here. On the contrary, it might be better to say that they accept our gaze without any resistance, and after sucking it in, they simply return to their state of silence. These mundane, all-too-mundane things and their fine detail lack any sort of symbolism or metaphor. The expression "the thing as it is" is far too vague. It points to the idea that the unmediated mixture of human consciousness and things (or nature) can sometimes dissolve the tense relationship between things as things, and consciousness as consciousness on the other side, but even so, when I look at Walker Evans's photographs, all I can express is the thing as it is; on my side, I can only become conscious of my own loss for words.

In every sense, Walker Evans's photographs strip away the anecdotal. He does away, too, with the formulaic method of the anecdote that has been used in our consciousness. This method attempts to explain a single actuality or situation by getting close to it; this proximity is generated by borrowing an already fixed way of speaking about a thing or situation, and placing these two in correspondence. Such a method becomes clear when one looks at other documents made through photography in the 1930s of cities, villages, and the people living in them, in particular the document-photographs of Dorothea Lange. A photograph considered to be one of Dorothea Lange's masterworks is a close-up of a middle-aged woman, gaze angled off to the side, who is embracing a young child. From the deep wrinkles carved into her forehead and her anxious eyes, this is certainly a document, not something that was fabricated. Even so, this photograph speaks only of that which is implied by the word *poverty*. The image is grasped from within the word, and loops back on itself. That is why it comforts people, in a certain sense. If *comfort* is perhaps not the proper word, then we could say that our consciousness remains unbothered, or that we are not led toward anxiety. The image becomes *nameable*; then, we are relieved.

However, Evans's photographs reject such naming. Well, perhaps it is too much to say that they "reject" it. Even if one tries to name them, they seep out of the frame that their naming would provide. Our gaze does not pierce Evans's photographs and the things that are captured in them, but rather passes straight through to the other side of these things. The only thing that makes it possible for a gaze to stabilize itself as a gaze is for there to be a time when it converges on a point somewhere on the object, rebounds, and then returns to some point in our consciousness. This makes it possible to maintain a stable relation between the thing (the world) and the self.

Evans endangers this relation itself. Before Walker Evans's photographs, our gaze is simply held in the state of having been emitted; it is impossible to know where it goes. The gaze is left hanging in midair.

Now, I am writing this based only on my distant memory; I am not looking at a single one of Walker Evans's photographs. For some reason, I think this seems proper in the case of Evans. This is because the vagueness or uncertainty of memory connects to the uncertainty of his images. (Needless to say, it is not the case that the things captured in Evans's photographs are unclear; on the contrary, his images are of almost extreme clarity.) Still, from within that vague memory, I am able to haul in a single photograph. It depicts a number of daily objects, including a used toothbrush, that sit on a crossbeam in an abandoned house. The photograph is taken straight on, from a middle distance. It is easy to give this photograph a meaning: the daily objects in a farmhouse that a family had to abandon because they became poor have been left just in the place where they had been used, and at the same time, they have been eaten away by time. Daily life rots away as part of daily life. Perhaps this family, like the main characters of *The Grapes of Wrath*, was incorporated into a city as part of the ranks of would-be industrial workers. It would be possible to go this far, through the interpretive flights of fancy at which we are so adept. But if we go there, just what does that do?

Nothing more is in front of me than a wall and crossbeam that make no attempt to speak of anything, and an old, used-up toothbrush.

Walker Evans's photographs do not reduce things—things as tools, things as their everyday meaning, in other words things as we are accustomed to them, and therefore things that are not wrapped up in any sort of doubt—to a different form, or take up the gesture of piercing us, or pushing themselves on us. They simply stare silently at everyday things from a certain distance, showing us their forms as they are. Everyday life is simply cut out as everyday life, and presented as that thing alone. They demand the return of everyday life as everyday life. This actually makes us anxious. The aesthetic *objet*, for instance when it takes on a strange form, does not threaten anyone. Ordinary abnormalities are given a stable position at the border of the vastness of the everyday. The two sides complement each other.

To speak only in terms of photography, Edward Weston's enlarged peppers or Bill Brandt's distorted nudes add up to nothing more than visual play. But in the case of Evans and Eugène Atget, who was so far away from Evans in time and space, their photographs lead us to anxiety in the most basic meaning of this word. Anxiety has no relation to simple fear. It shakes the relation between the self and the world, and is born out of a distortion in this relation that one day suddenly swoops down upon us. Walker Evans's photographs are among the very few that have produced such anxiety in me.

The silence of Evans's photographs unexpectedly compels us to fill it in with language. But even if one had tens of thousands of words, this would probably not be enough. Words pass straight through Evans's things, end up somewhere, and disappear. The toothbrush, the old commemorative photograph on the wall, the grave mound exposed to the sun—all of these things appear before my eyes, and only I remain, looking at them. Right back at the beginning.

It is said that Walker Evans took these photographs alongside Dorothea Lange and Ben Shahn, who later became a famous painter, under the photography program of the FSA (Farm Security Administration), a part of the 1930s New Deal that sought to fight against the impoverishment of farming villages. I do not know whether Evans took photographs before this. Then again, perhaps the question of whether or not Evans was a photographer is irrelevant. Just like the old pinned-up commemorative photograph—the photograph in the photograph—that was taken by somebody, the things that have been transposed and fixed here seem to wait in eternal silence in the hope of being named. At the very least, when I see a photograph that is said to be taken by Evans, I feel such a thing.

First published in the photography magazine *Asahi Camera*, July 1975. Later collected in *Duel on Photography* (coauthored with Kishin Shinoyama, Asahi Shimbunsha, 1977).

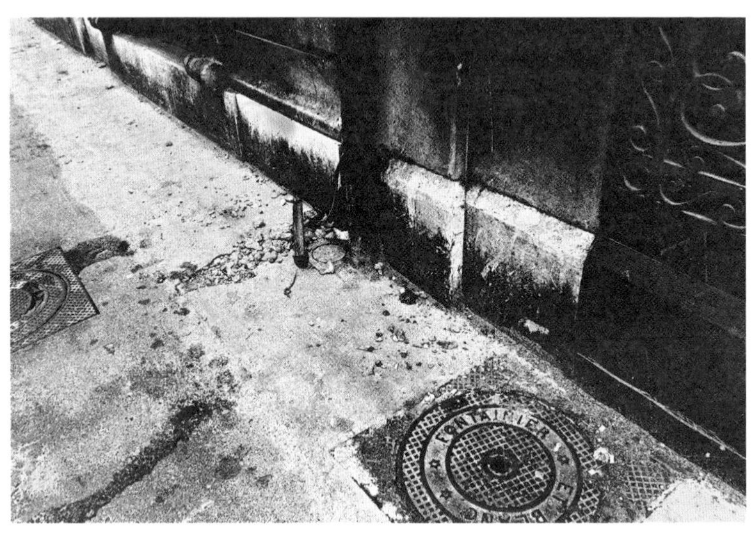

Takuma Nakahira, *The Streets, or Traces of Terror*, Marseille, 1976

The Will Toward History: Surrealism's Potential Power

It remains unclear whether the Surrealist movement should be spoken of as a "movement" with a definite idea. To be sure, Surrealism was a "movement" in terms of its form. This is quite obvious if one considers the Manifesto of Surrealism of 1924, the Second Manifesto of Surrealism of 1930, and the various other manifestos released by the Surrealists, who passionately affirmed that they were pushing forward a single "movement." However, when considering the transformations over time of its leader André Breton and the diversity of his reactions to reality, the multiplicity of its members, the subtle differences in the way that each of them responded to reality, and the ebb and flow of these members, Surrealism might be too diffuse to be seen as a "movement." Instead, it might be taken as the tremendous diffusion and dissipation of a nebulous energy, so to speak. In fact, in a narrow sense, Surrealism is the almost physiologically raw rejection and critique of reality by European intellectuals and artists in the 1930s and 1940s, and in that sense, it might be correct to say that Surrealism is like a convulsive spasm. And it is precisely for this reason that it could possess a certain power, or at least a potential power.

The end of World War I saw the establishment of the Versailles system; Stalin's betrayal of the Russian Revolution; the rise of emergent fascism; the Spanish Civil War; and the first omens of World War II. It also saw the "decline of the West," through the stirrings of the "Third World." If one asks precisely when the period that is contemporary in every sense began, this question could surely be answered in various ways. However, at the very least, one could venture to say that this period in fact marks the beginning of the contemporary. Important contemporary questions were already here: the domination of humans by modern technology, the unending menace of war, the exposure of the absolute inability of Stalinism to oppose it, the difficulty of contemporary revolution, and the somewhat desperate attempts to get beyond this difficulty. The Surrealists faced up to all of this at once, and they were able to take it on precisely because they were so earnest. While at times the Surrealists showed a somewhat childish rejection of reality, a rebellion for rebellion's sake, this does not speak of self-indulgence as much as it attests to their earnestness and acute instincts. The Surrealists of the 1920s and 1930s survive for us today as an aborted brother precisely because, through the sublime quality of this rejection—and certainly not in any sense of political validity—they open up the contemporary. More than anything, what we carry on today is not the actual substance of what the movement of Surrealism took on in its time, but the will toward history of "total revolt," "complete insubordination," "sabotage according to rule," and "violence."[1] In that sense, the Surrealists of the 1920s and 1930s are revolutionaries born well ahead of their time, who correctly saw the orientation of contemporary revolution but were also unable to find the method that would have allowed them to realize it within the structure of reality that is history. Here we might sense a certain "tragic" echo. But to lift them up as "tragic" heroes would be to bury Surrealism among the relics of "history." Within our own historical moment, the important thing to ask is to what extent we inherit the questions that they raised. This is the only way to rescue Surrealism as a will toward history from Surrealism as a mode of cutting-edge design within genres of individual expression like poetry, literature, and painting.

"Everything tends to make us believe that there exists a certain point of the mind at which life and death, the real and the imagined, past and future, the communicable and the incommunicable, high and low, cease to be perceived as contradictions."[2] Aside from this extremely famous assertion of Breton's, which dissolves such fusions, the logic of a thorough "negation" holds across Surrealist thought. This can be seen in the continued opposition of dreams and the imagination to the utility of reality ("Beloved imagination, what I most like in you is your unsparing quality," First Manifesto); of the unknown to the known ("Let us not mince words: the marvelous is always beautiful, anything marvelous is beautiful, in fact only the marvelous is beautiful," First Manifesto); of the unconscious to the conscious (the self); of play to labor; of wildness to reason; of childhood to adulthood; and of violence to obedience.[3] To be sure, as a defiant gesture, Breton's refusal burned beautifully at first, like a beacon. Such antithesis is the first step of defiance or rebellion, and today it is taken for granted, or better, it has acquired even more validity as a real and concrete historical task. However, in 1920s and 1930s Europe, such an extremely rushed antithesis was bound to gradually disengage from reality. At a certain point, the thesis that needed to dialectically oppose the antithesis did not arrive; from then on things could only acquire a certain mystical coloration. Or perhaps not that—the Surrealists knew the dialectic that one needs to live out. But because they could not find a material base within the world, their dialectic could only come to naught. In other words, while the Surrealists correctly called for nothing other than to unify the revolutions of spirit and matter, the simultaneous progression of these two revolutions (the challenge that we face today in our own cultural revolution) was dismissed as too sudden by the subjects of proletarian revolution who the Surrealists were ready to "serve" for that purpose.

"How can one accept the fact that the dialectical method can only be validly applied to the solution of social problems?"[4] "I really fail to see—some narrow-minded revolutionaries notwithstanding—why we should refrain from supporting the Revolution, provided we view the problems of love, dreams, madness, art, and religion from the same angle they do."[5] Breton *did really fail to see this*. But history has drastic stages. The proletariat—the subject of Marxist revolution—and the Communist parties of various countries under the self-proclaimed "correct" revolutionary party of Stalin grounded themselves in the expansion of production, and in dismantling repressive modes of production. In other words, the sole content of revolution was designated as the proletariat seizing power. This was the absolute priority of material revolution. It was not doubted for an instant that the revolution of consciousness, of the unconscious—in short, the revolution of culture—would come later, some day after the material revolution was accomplished, as a kind of grace. The proletariat accepted this thesis almost entirely in full, and at that historical stage it could not see the proposals of Breton and company. Exposed to a kind of reverse illumination from this undeniable fact, the proposals of Surrealism appeared dreamy; the proletariat could only view one side, their emphasis on the "internal," making it inevitable that they became shrouded in a veneer of mysticism. As a result, Surrealism had to shoulder the fate of distortion and transformation that emerged through determinations made separately from the claims of Breton and his group. As a matter of course, this reality forced Surrealism to isolate itself, and enclose itself within a small movement of a few intellectuals. This situation is precisely what later made Surrealism a target of criticism by those who took it as a kind of enemy. "Actually, it is the mysticism without God which demonstrates and quenches the rebel's thirst for the absolute."[6] (Albert Camus) "Too well-mannered to kill everybody, the surrealists, by the very logic of their attitude, came to consider that, in order to liberate desire, society must first be overthrown. They chose to serve the revolutionary movement of their times."[7] Even further, in the first section of *The Rebel*, Camus rejects Surrealist rebellion on the grounds that it proposes a "metaphysical rebellion" which is then followed by "historical rebellion."[8] This almost entirely reverses what Breton and other Surrealists had set out to do.

Still, leaving Breton aside for the moment, it cannot be said that the Surrealists never carried out actions that deserve such criticism. As much as the Surrealists' harsh rebellion against reality was meant to be a total one, and as much as they strengthened their will toward the total liberation of humanity, this was blocked by their present reality, and so as they sharpened and radicalized their "concepts," there was nothing left for them to do but preserve their own identity. The misfortune of history lies in the fact that the Surrealists had a correct and penetrating understanding of reality, but reality let them down all the same. Their frustration at this situation inevitably led them to purify the "concept" itself, by piling up "negation" upon "negation." Perhaps this is a biased view of the past seen as a bystander of the present day.

To take one example, we can see this in the activity and various political appeals of the revolutionary intellectual group Contre-Attaque, formed around Georges Bataille and André Breton, that existed for an extremely short time between late 1935 and the spring of 1936. This period is a decisive historical turning point. On the one hand, there was the threat of Nazism (Hitler had taken power in 1933); on the other, Stalin's declaration to "protect the fatherland," the signing of the Franco-Soviet Treaty of Mutual Assistance and, in response to this, the capitulation of the French Popular Front to the Stalinist line, thus decisively thwarting the revolution to come, and strangling the Spanish Revolution. Reality appeared in an extremely condensed form that rose up all at once. In response to such a raw reality, the Surrealists took their own raw counterposition. In practice, the activity of Contre-Attaque was an intense but all too brief movement. However, for better or worse, this momentary brilliance vividly illustrates the true radicalism of the Surrealist movement. I will cite below some of the appeals of Contre-Attaque, in order to sum up their important points:[9]

> To severely oppose any sort of tendency, whatever form it may take, that attempts to coax revolution toward the concept of the country or the fatherland.

For those determined to seize power, a *domineering violence* that surpasses any other form of violence is necessary.

The leaders of the Popular Front will likely approach power within the framework of the bourgeois system, but we now declare that such a program is on the verge of bankruptcy. To establish political and public security for the people, *a firm dictatorship by the armed people is necessary*.

We enter the ranks of workers, and appeal to their supremely bold and ambitious craving, a craving that cannot be fulfilled within the framework of the current society. Without prostrating ourselves before anything, we appeal to their *human instincts*, their moral freedom, and *their violence*.

That is why this time, *we must use the weapon created by fascism, which was able to exploit the fundamental human craving for emotional exaltation and fanaticism, on our own side*.

These declarations themselves were drafted by Georges Bataille. Bataille's own personality is strongly reflected here. One could say that in the phrases I emphasized—"domineering violence," "the fundamental human craving for emotional exaltation and fanaticism"—Bataille's decisive pessimism has turned back on itself, and become a kind of Bolshevism of sentiment. Be that as it may, one can clearly see a similar consciousness in the Surrealists' own recognition of reality, for example in André Breton's criticism of the PCF, which bent to Stalin's declaration and suddenly introduced the term "fatherland": "We Surrealists 'don't love our country.'"[10] He sternly protested against the PCF's use of the term "fatherland" to gin up support against Nazism and suppress the revolution of the Popular Front, all to preserve the existing bourgeois democratic system: "We will oppose it insofar as it might serve to sanction the feeling that there will inevitably be a war that French workers would be all the happier to leave for because they would be preceded not only by the tricolor, but by *the tricolor and the red flag*."[11] (These citations come from the text of a speech for the "Congress of Writers for the Defense of Culture"; Breton was prevented from actually delivering this speech himself because of the famous "Ehrenburg Incident.") This was a desperate attempt to rescue a true revolution from the Stalinist abandonment of revolution, from the distortion of Marxist political theory, and from all other stifled versions of revolution that would continue to spring forth afterward. In principle, the Surrealists completely saw through the division and reorganization of friends and enemies. But once history is distorted, that distortion begins to acquire necessity. The Surrealists swore their loyalty to Marxism, even if this meant going overboard, or sometimes going so far as to obliterate themselves. However, Moscow decisively undercut the proletariat, to whom the Surrealists' dreams had been entrusted. Surrealism's fundamentally antifascist, anti-imperialist, and anti-Stalinist "revolution" could find no foothold in reality; it was driven into the position of a "conceptual," "metaphysical" rebellion for an absolute minority. Faced with blind obedience to the reality principle or enclosing themselves within the fortress of the pleasure principle, which must always be suppressed, the Surrealists chose the latter. This meant exposing themselves to an unceasing "negation" that lacked the fundamental dialectic between reality and pleasure principles, a pseudo-dialectic in which sometimes the backside of the backside simply became the front.

Georges Bataille took this to an extreme. "A fanatical, rising, and violent movement that emerges from the people's ill will—a movement that is free of the sterile control of all parties, is made up of *volunteer soldiers for freedom*—this is truly the basic condition of seizing power. When the armed ill will of the masses arising from the Popular Front provides an unrelenting foundation for authority, power will belong to the revolution." Contre-Attaque, which was centered around Bataille, went even further. It cried out for the rejection of all forms of power, including the morality toward one's parents (opposed by the adventure and play of children), the fatherland (opposed by the continent), and even the power of revolution itself. It was for Fourier's fantasies, Nietzsche's "corruption," Sade's atheism. And also: "Rather, we prefer, *above all else* and without being deceived, Hitler's anti-diplomatic crudeness, which is clearly less harmful than the greedy enticements of diplomats and politicians."[12]

By the time it came this far, Surrealism was practically standing back-to-back with nihilism. It was trying to preserve the correctness of what it had been aiming for, but its failure to grasp concrete strategies and tactics within the dynamics of history led, at that time, to the bankruptcy of Surrealist "revolution." Surrealism regressed all the way back to its progenitor, Dada. It even began to show an animosity toward the proletariat, who it had simply assumed would be on its side. "The simplest Surrealist act consists of dashing down into the street, pistol in hand, and firing blindly, as fast as you can pull the trigger, into the crowd."[13] In such a reality, this extremely famous metaphor got a new lease on life—but this time, in the concrete place of politics. Surrealism failed to grasp reality and carry out its "revolution" within it, so it took on the guise of an absolutist rebel, all or nothing, and was decisively boxed in by history. Their slogans of anti-Stalinism, anti-imperialism, and antifascism remained correct at that time, just as they remain correct today. But the only factor that lets correctness appear as correctness is the given historical situation—and this is what gives the Surrealists their clumsy gait, their sad *grimace*.

Fundamentally, Surrealism was an attempt at the total liberation of the human. This is why it was the first shot fired against the logic of positivism, which supports the modern system of capital. For the painters and poets, this meant destroying existing forms of art, and a deepening of recognition through a fusion of science and poetry in which, to borrow Breton's words, "no means has been designated a priori."[14] This deepening of recognition would produce the liberation of the human. Freud's reliance on the return of dreams and imagination also springs from this point. In other words, it is an attempt to completely reconsider reality as it had existed until that point. Perhaps it would be better to call it the simultaneous transformation of self and reality. The Surrealist poetic technique of automatism, too, was intended to disturb the stability of the self, and stir up consciousness through the abruptness of the unconscious. At a time when language was already becoming a form of suppression, automatism was thought up as a way to demolish this very language, and then bring it back to life. Breton consistently discusses keeping the self as receptive as possible, and the "Surrealist method of composing words," of simply waiting for the unconscious to arise; Bataille argues for "the rejection of choice"; and Hofmannsthal, who Bataille himself cites, says: "It is not that the poet thinks ceaselessly of all the things in the world; they think of him. They are in him, they dominate him."[15] These are serious efforts to work toward a renewed grasp of the world and the human, by clearing away the modern dualism of ego and world from its greatest depths.

Therefore, or because of this, the Surrealists cleared away the systematized isolation of poetry and painting, and worked to make "transforming the world" (Marx) and "changing life" (Rimbaud) into one thing. This was their one and only method for the liberation of the human.

The Surrealists demanded infinite freedom of thought, yet believed in social revolution through dialectical materialism. To bring their initial project to fruition, they stood in between these two things that, in concrete terms, are incompatible; they went through various trials and errors, and they did not hesitate to try out things that looked like compromises. Breton joined the Communist Party, left it, then became almost a kind of supplicant to Trotsky after Stalin exiled the latter. These movements certainly leave behind a zigzag pattern. But they speak to the temporary setbacks of a cultural revolution that aimed for and failed to achieve (because it had come all too early) the liberation of the human through the twinned liberations of sensation and society.

The traces left behind by Surrealism in the first quarter of this century continue to offer us clues for our own liberation today.

It is said that Surrealism suddenly came back to life on the streets of Paris in May 1968. This time, right in the heart of a highly managed society, the rebellious gestures of anonymous students and workers directed against that society brought it back to life. This feels somewhat ironic, because although early Surrealism declared that anyone could be a poet, regardless of talent, it is also undeniable that their somewhat absurd actions were eventually transformed, as a new fashion, into bourgeois objects of comfort. The will toward history of Surrealism as a cultural revolution suffered a temporary setback before. But if it has now thrown off the shackles of artistic formalism with which it was saddled, and revived itself, this would actually prove in reverse that Surrealism during the 1920s and 1930s possessed a vast potential power.

Today, capitalism has taken on its final form of the highly managed society, or "consumer society." The distortions and the high degree of systematization produced by managed national monopoly capitalism go all the way to structure the instincts of each person living in this system. They shape the most physiological parts of the human; in other words, desire itself is shaped in accordance with them, to produce a desire that allows for the easy reception of commodities. There is no longer anything like the desire of the people in and of itself, much less a revolutionary desire. When we clearly see that, on the contrary, desire now helps to reproduce the system, we must accept the Surrealist thesis of carrying out the simultaneous revolutions of human sensation and society together as something real. Nothing would change if the "proletariat"—in which the seeds of ill desire, ill sensation have been planted at will—were to simply take the reins of power. That is not revolution, or anything of the sort. It is just a changing of the guard. Precisely because of this, the revelations of Surrealism can finally appear before our eyes today as concrete challenges for human liberation.

"'Power to the people' does not mean the (anything but 'silent') majority of the population as it exists today; it means a minority. . . . However, the ambivalence of the slogan expresses the truth that 'the people,' the majority of the people are *de facto*, *distinct from*, and *apart from* their government, that self-government of the people is still to be fought for. It means that this goal *pre*supposes a radical change in the needs and consciousness of the people" (Herbert Marcuse).[16] The "*distinct from*" that is spoken of here, the "radical change in the needs and consciousness of the people": this is the practical context that connects Breton's call for "changing the world" and "changing life" to our reality.

First published in the art magazine *Bijutsu Techō*, December 1975.

Notes

1 André Breton, "Second Manifesto of Surrealism [1930]," in *Manifestoes of Surrealism*, trans. Richard Seaver and Helen R. Lane (Ann Arbor: University of Michigan Press, 1972), 125.

2 Breton, "Second Manifesto of Surrealism," 123. Not cited by Nakahira in the original text.

3 André Breton, "Manifesto of Surrealism [1924]," in *Manifestoes of Surrealism*, trans. Richard Seaver and Helen R. Lane (Ann Arbor: University of Michigan Press, 1972), 4, 14.

4 Breton, "Second Manifesto of Surrealism," 140.

5 Ibid.

6 Albert Camus, *The Rebel*, trans. Anthony Bower (New York: Vintage Books, 1956), 97–98.

7 Ibid., 94.

8 These are the titles of parts 2 and 3 of Camus's book.

9 Throughout the essay, Nakahira quotes Japanese translations by French literary scholar Kunio Iwaya of documents related to Contre-Attaque that ran in the Japanese magazine *Paideia*, no. 8 (August 1970): 35–55. Since no English translations of these documents have been published, we have translated Iwaya's translations into English. With the exception of the third quote, all emphasis is added by Nakahira.

10 PCF refers to the Parti communiste français (French Communist Party). André Breton, "Speech to the Congress of Writers [1935]," in *Manifestoes*

of Surrealism, trans. Richard Seaver and Helen R. Lane (Ann Arbor: University of Michigan Press, 1972), 237.

11 Ibid., 237, 238.

12 The quotes attributed to Bataille in this paragraph come from the Japanese translations that appeared in the August 1970 issue of *Paideia*.

13 Breton, "Second Manifesto of Surrealism," 125.

14 Breton, "Manifesto of Surrealism," 10. Not cited by Nakahira in the original text.

15 Nakahira does not cite Breton or Bataille. The Hofmannsthal quote appears in Maurice Blanchot, *The Space of Literature* (Lincoln: University of Nebraska Press, 1982), 179. Blanchot's text was translated into Japanese in *Paideia*, no. 6 (August 1969).

16 Herbert Marcuse, *Counterrevolution and Revolt* (Boston: Beacon Press, 1972), 46.

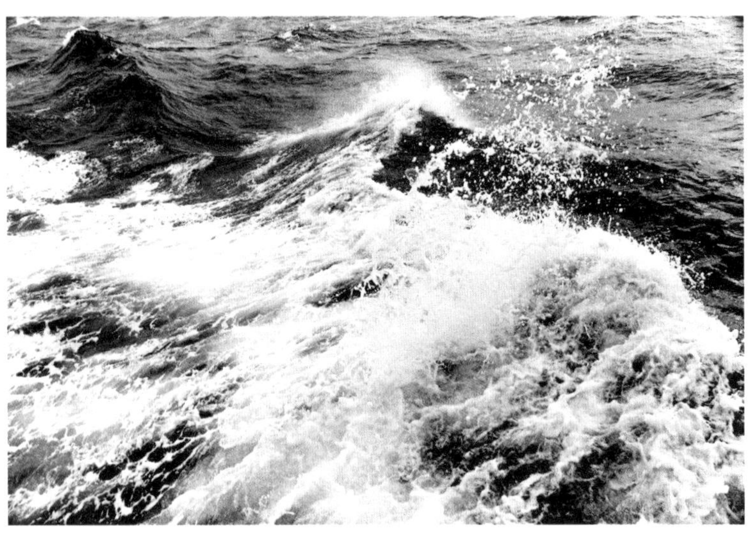

Takuma Nakahira, *Tokara Islets*, 1976

Interlude

The sun was trying to set slowly. No sign of anyone on the beach on this late fall evening. I sprinkled some gasoline and lit a match. Everything started burning up at once, and a strong flame shot into the air. Black smoke wrapped the outer circumference of the flame. No wind, I thought. But the flame swayed from side to side, like a twisted column. An unexpectedly strong wind blew in from the sea, hit the cliff, split in two, and swirled together here. The frenzy of a local wind. Or maybe the flame had quickly warmed the air, and the wind was produced here. As the blaze rocked back and forth, I had to change the position of my body. The fire, which had looked vigorous, started to cool down. Only the black smoke was getting bigger. The fire just glided across the surface; only the gasoline was burning. I picked up a piece of driftwood that had been wet by the lapping waves. It was just thick enough to fit in the palm of my hand. I poked the base of the fire with it. This split the black lump that was blocking the flames. I felt the fire regain its steady force. This would do.

I thought that the wind had gotten weaker. The sun had already completely disappeared beneath the horizon. Still, it was strangely bright. This small beach: a cape to the right that described a slow arc of about one kilometer, beyond that a jetty made of tetrapods, and some artificial land on which a few houses had started to be built. And then, standing alone, this small beach. There was usually always someone taking a walk before dinner, or people casting and reeling for sand whitings. But on this day, there was absolutely no sign of anyone. Perhaps it was too late to take a walk, or perhaps the cold snap that came in the previous night drove everyone away.

Even as the fire became weaker or stronger, it maintained a steady burn. The waves were calmly rising and crashing. A wave rises up slowly, and for an instant, at the peak, appears to stand still. At this time, the water of the ocean, at its most intense transparency, produces the most material-like sensation of heaviness. In the next moment, the wave tries to lift itself up, cannot bear the force, and breaks apart. A monotonous, swooning kind of repetition. All I could hear were the sounds of this fire burning in the dusk, and this rising and crashing of waves. It had been ten, or no, maybe twenty minutes since I lit the fire. The fire was burning well. In an instant, the fire lifted up the pages of a notebook. As they rose up and curled, the fleeting white space of the notebook emphasized the encroaching darkness that surrounded it. The poorly written letters were small, densely packed in, rounded. I could read some fragments. "All the leaves turn yellow . . ." "Oh fallen leaves, . . . come." A quotation of some kind. "Nibrol, six tablets"; "Two decanters of sake, insomnia medicine."[1] Random characters entered my eyes. It was impossible to read through everything. As the flame fanned over the white pages, the area around it turned dark brown. The dark brown invaded the white and swiftly turned it gray. With the small swirls of air that blew the flame around, the page shriveled, burned up, became light. Then, it became a brittle lump and rolled away. Underneath it, the next page appeared. The flame carefully went through each page, one by one. "Tri-X, F11, 1/250." Shooting data. "As much as one might dig up . . . just like the larva of a beetle . . ." Memories came up one after the other.

The fire burned with its own power. I no longer needed the beer bottle filled with gasoline that I had prepared, it shouldn't catch on fire, I suddenly thought. Take the beer bottle with gasoline and go home ahead of me, I said to my wife. I stayed fixated on the flame. Looking closely, there was a blueish part in the middle of the otherwise all-red flame. For some reason, this part was the most aggressive. The fire within the fire, that kind of feeling. The blue flame split up into smaller flames, and each part of this squadron attacked the individual pages of the notebook. There was something ferocious about this. There was almost no smoke there; it was transparent like the flame of a gas burner. The black smoke only appeared somewhere at the top of the fire, after it had first become part of the red flame.

The fire shook violently again. I was flustered, and jerked my upper body back. I changed the position of my body. My eye was drawn to the small blue flames pushing through the notebook. They looked carefree, but they were burning steadily. Several notebooks had already been consumed. Above the paper that had become black ash, some white, almost silver characters floated up. They were fanned by the wind, sent flying by the flame, and went off in all directions. A wreckage of meaning was strewn above this rustling ash that could no longer be called paper. The fire continued to burn. But now the thick bundle of film was blocking it. The flames went around it, and looked like they were hesitating about where to start.

I felt someone's presence and took my eyes off the fire. An old man was standing. On the other side of the fire, about two meters away, an old man stood. I did not know when he appeared, or where he came from. I turned away and looked at the ocean, then at the sky. The dusk continued as before. Not too much time has passed, I thought to myself. I recalled learning the etymology of the word *twilight* [*tasogare*].[2] The moment of twilight stretched on for eternity, sticking to the sky and the ocean. The waves lapped and lapped against the shore. The old man spoke to me in a quiet voice. Without catching any meaning, I nodded vaguely. He was a small and thin old man. In his dark face, only his eyes shone. He looked fifty, but he also looked seventy. His appearance was rough. Seeing me nod, the old man started to burn something in the fire.

My eyes went back to the fire. The bundle of film was smoldering, and now started to emit black smoke. Various columns of black smoke ran parallel to each other. I poked the fire with a stick and pried it open. As much as possible, I tried to separate each roll of film. The negative holders burned first. But the fire suddenly weakened when it reached the film itself. The edge of the film bent slightly, but did not catch. The blue flames persistently attacked it. An acrid, sour smell began to fill the air. I did not know whether it was coming from the film or from something the old man was burning on the fire.

Over a long time, the film burned. Or no, rather, it simmered, so that it all fused together into a single puddle. Each roll of film clearly went, one by one. I'll get every last roll this way, I thought. I did not think about what I was doing this for. Or, I thought about it for an instant, and then stopped thinking. The old man dragged something from the fire and stubbed it out with the sole of his shoe. Sometimes he spoke to me. As before, I understood nothing. I don't need to understand, I thought. He was in a good mood. For no reason, this irritated me. You're the only one talking here, pal, I said without forming a sound. Or perhaps a small sound did come out. The old man was carefully collecting cinders on one part of the beach. He had found some copper wires somewhere, and was burning off the rubber. He was bending the exposed wires into a lump.

When his work had finished, the old man produced a large bottle from his bag, and took a swig of the liquid inside. He did not seem about to get up and leave. On the contrary, he skillfully separated out the bundle of film and adjusted the firewood, so that the fire started burning again. He was used to working with fire. His methods were those of a pro. With the old man's touch, all of a sudden the negatives started to burn well. I thought that all of my efforts up to now were foolish. Everything had been futile. You didn't have to make a fool of me, I thought, and I was filled with an outlandish anger. At the same time, I had the reckless feeling, go on then, do it yourself.

What are you burning, the old man asked. This time I could hear his voice clearly. I'm burning photographs, I said. Why are you burning photographs, came the reply. Because I'm a photographer, I said. Why does a photographer burn photographs, he should have asked. Pro photographers burn photographs, I was going to answer. But he did not ask anything more. As if to say he understood everything, the old man continued deftly burning the negatives. While doing this, he took another swig of the liquid in the bottle. I was annoyed that the question I expected did not emerge. I knew that the unhappiness I had felt just before would return.

The bundle of black-and-white prints also caught fire, and each print curled up and burned crisply. With each one, memories were summoned back to me. It was all so raw. In the moment that each photograph burned, I recalled with overly detailed clarity everything about when, where, and how I had taken it.

Heading down the Tōmei Expressway, around two in the morning, parked off to the side, I set my camera on a guardrail and took a long exposure, four or five seconds, of the Fuji Industrial Complex. I remembered a hot and humid night in August 1969. A, the young guy who always drove me. I hadn't seen him for a long time now. The landscape of the Fuji Industrial Complex, burning in the night sky, was now burning up in front of my eyes, engulfed in flames. Golden Gai, near where the Shinjuku streetcars had once run. Only the rusted rails were left, and in the middle of an endless night of wandering, drinking, and throwing up on the street, I took a photograph of those rails and a distant figure. The emphasized perspective of a 28mm wide lens. The city melting into darkness. After two straight sleepless nights, I went to M's house in Musashi-Koyama and passed out like a dead weight in the monsoon season afternoon. When my eyes opened, M was gone. I stepped out into the evening city under a light rain, and my eye happened to stop on a wreath of flowers to celebrate the opening of a pachinko parlor. Drops of rain on the clear bag covering the wreath. They were plastic flowers that looked far more flower-like than flowers. Like it was yesterday, I recalled clicking the shutter over and over, adjusting my angle a little bit each time.

One by one, all of the human relations around these photographs go up in flames before my eyes. They become ash. The relationships distort, curl up, burn up in an instant, disappear. By now, I finally started to feel like I understood why I was burning my notebooks, burning the writing I'd done in various places, and burning my photographs. I had no idea what I would do after this. But I will never take a photograph again, I thought. I cannot become a collector of memories, I thought. "Every detail has the same quality as the totality." Exactly. But, then what? "Dialectical thinking is . . ." "The critical tension between 'it is' and 'it should be'" "it, firstly . . ." Knowledge is of no help at all in facing up to this reality. It is no more than a ball and chain.

The old man had already turned almost everything to ash. At some point he had produced a poker in his left hand. The tension of the muscles in his left arm suddenly came into my eyes. His veins turned dark red, and the tension passed through his elbow to his fist. This hand was holding a piece of driftwood. For such a small man, he had unusually large arms and hands. Had these hands done karate? Boxing? Or something else? For some reason, they gave me a lewd feeling.

I clearly heard the voice of a woman: "Hey, come home, quick." I thought I heard it. Of course, I was only hearing things. That's right, the old man had taken away my last chance. With his dark hands, he had taken away even my last chance. He raised the bottle to his lips again. As if caring for the fire, he moved the embers around with the driftwood.

I suddenly felt cold. The fire had already turned into a source of heat. I now knew that there was alcohol in the bottle. What is that, I asked. Saying nothing, the old man passed the bottle over the embers. This is the best flavor, he said. He had a slight Tōhoku accent. In the bottle was finely chopped garlic, on top of which *shōchū* had been poured. Looking through the fire, about 1.5 or 2 centimeters of garlic had sunk to the bottom, a third of the bottle.

The minced garlic floated in the half-translucent liquid like muck. Filthy, I thought. But my desire to get drunk was stronger. It was a big bottle that held cheap whiskey before. I quickly took a drink, trying as much as possible to have my lips avoid the mouth of the bottle. The smell of *shōchū* and garlic spread throughout my mouth. My throat made a move to wretch it up. I forced it down. I felt the alcohol swirling around inside my stomach.

Night had completely fallen on the beach. The whites of the breaking waves were within reach. The sea was at a lull. I saw lapping waves. High tide was near. I felt a chemical sort of heat spreading from my stomach to all parts of my body. This made me feel the cold outside once again. I took another gulp. There was no longer any nausea. The stars were not out. I heard the horn of a car in the distance. I thought a little about my wife and child. My wife had taken the beer bottle filled with gasoline and headed home. Around this time, she would probably be preparing dinner for my son. She, the child, and our cat, Nekosu, lived with a single steady rhythm. My son does not know why our cat has this name. This is from when he was still small, just before entering preschool. There was a time when he would go around the city deciphering the letters he had just learned. We would drive around. My son sat in the passenger seat and read off just the *hiragana* letters of public transport signs or billboards. In a loud voice, without any context, he would read: "*Sa*,"or "*wo*, *ikema*, *sen*." It was funny. *Katakana* letters came a little after, I guess. There was a factory for chairs, or something like that, next to the tracks of the suburban railroad, and the word *Nekosu* was written in large letters there. At some point my son memorized this word and lumped it together with *neko*, the word for cat. From that point on, all of his cats have been called Nekosu. Their daily life had a clear rhythm. The daily life of two people and one animal.

"Do not enter into that tender night." Those words unexpectedly floated up. Perhaps it was "do not enter tender into that night." Still, I did not know whose phrase this was, whether it was the title of a novel, or a line from a poem.[3] I looked up at the pitch-black sky. My eyes slowly moved downwards. The darkness ran straight down from the sky, all the way to the barely glimmering white of the waves.

There was no boundary between the sea and the sky, just the jet-black celestial sphere. Depending on the fire, the profile of the old man rose up hazily from time to time. I could tell that he was very drunk. He sat on some dry sand, and looked like he was going to cross his legs. He continued to mutter. His voice was low and gravelly. I couldn't grasp most of what he was saying. It seemed like he was talking to himself, anyway. My wife couldn't put up with me, and the kids are just kids. At least that he spoke clearly, it seemed. He continued talking to himself for a while. Then, suddenly, Mao Zedong is great. Then he said names that were either Chinese or Vietnamese. Mr. Li, Mr. Pan, Mr. Pao, Mr. Chu, all Vietnamese people are good, he said. Oh, so you also invaded China, and fled south when you were defeated, did you? I was filled with anger. What's all this about Mao Zedong? Why Mao Zedong? No drifter's going to lecture me! But the old man did not respond. Everything after that was incoherent.

The old man looked like he was getting more and more drunk. Over half of the bottle was already empty. The fire got smaller. The old man stood up and disappeared into the darkness. Then he quickly came back with some driftwood or small bamboo, and a box for beer bottles. He piled up the wood, and put the bamboo inside. The fire rose up. The warmth came back again. I drew my hand to the bottle, which was next to the old man, and drank without a word. I felt liquid spill out of my mouth, run across my cheek, and go into my long hair. The old man didn't say anything. The taste was beside the point. I just thought the old man shouldn't get drunk by himself. The old man started up again. My wife won't put up with me, and the kids following her are just kids. I have a kid too, pal, you're not the only one! Not all kids are good-for-nothings like yours! Instead of saying that, I drank from the nearly empty bottle, fueled by the petty feeling that I would refuse to pass it back to the old man. I could feel my intoxication. It felt incredibly comfortable. The old man picked out pieces of garlic from the now-empty bottle with his finger and transferred them to his mouth. He was using his right hand. This hand, and its fingers, were both small and dainty. Just like a shrimp. I thought of the figure of a large snapping shrimp, with one enlarged claw, that I had seen in one of my child's illustrated guides. There was no end in sight to the old man's mutterings. So, you'll go on continuing to curse at your wife and child while saying Mao Zedong is great? And you plan to just settle on into that like you sat down here? Your trifling Mao Zedong is a piece of shit. And your trifling wife, and your good-for-nothing urchin, too.

For some reason, from within my clouded consciousness, I suddenly realized that I needed to properly extinguish the fire. Again without reason, I thought that I would need to burn everything up, or make sure that no trace would be left. Like a criminal. Thinking like this made things somewhat funny. I staggered up. Looking behind me, I saw that without a sound the waves had come within about two meters of me. They rose up and crashed. Nothing at all had changed from before. I just hadn't heard the sound. It was as if the ocean had risen to an abnormal level. The ocean and the beach mixed, melting into each other. The border was not fixed. On such a night, the giant oarfish slowly rises from the deep, with its large eyes like buttons.

I checked the remains of the fire. My feet staggered. The old man said nothing. He was sitting straight, with his legs crossed. Everything was burning beautifully. I carefully hit the fire with another piece of driftwood and stepped on it. There were no remains of film or prints or notebooks or drafts. I used an empty can that had rolled up to scoop up some seawater and sprinkle it around the edge of the fire. The fire smoked, and a cloud of ash rose up. At that time, I noticed a white piece of paper left on the sand, about three meters away from me. Just as I thought—best to be careful. It was a single black-and-white print. It must have fallen out before I started the fire, when I was bringing things over. A highway stretched out in a straight line, and beyond it, a row of public apartments seemed about to cover it up. Because of a mistake with the fixer, or a light leak while developing the film, the right half was discolored; it looked like a photomontage. I had taken it out of the front window of a car, on the way from Osaka to Himeji. I remembered seeing the ocean along the way, at Akashi. I had already heard about the pollution in the Seto Inland Sea. But the ocean at Akashi was clear and blue. When I was still a child I visited my aunt in Akashi, and I saw octopi hanging out to dry on a rack by the shore. The sun was bright, shining through the thin bodies of the octopi. That was my first memory of seeing the ocean. Perhaps I was four or five years old.

I held the photograph over the nearly extinguished fire. The fire caught the edge of the print, which started to burn. My fingers were hot. I waited as long as I could, and let it drop. I picked it up again, and let it go in the last part of the fire that was still burning. It burned quietly, and that was all. This time, I scooped up seawater with my hands and put it directly on the fire. I repeated this a few times. The fire was now completely out. White smoke like steam floated low across the wet sand. If I leave things like this, by tomorrow morning the ocean should wash everything away. It's a dark night, but it's definitely a full moon, I thought.

I thought I should go home, then suddenly realized I had nothing like a home to which I could go. A knothole, I thought. I'm a knothole in a storm door. Just like the lens of a camera obscura. Passing through me, the relation between the outside world and the world of my wife, child, and cat was like that between an image that is upside down and one that is right side up. I did not know which was which. If here is right side up then there is upside down; if here is upside down, then there is right side up. In any case, I am a knothole. A simple hole. A hole is not a being. I thought such things. Then I thought that this is all pure idealism, and laughed. My insides were drunk, but my skin had gotten chilly. Only my face was warm. I started to walk home. Soon enough, the tremendous hangover came. The old man was gone.

First published in the photography magazine *Asahi Camera*, July 1976. Later collected in *Duel on Photography* (coauthored with Kishin Shinoyama, Asahi Shimbunsha, 1977).

Notes

1 Nibrol is the name of a sleeping pill.

2 The term *tasogare* refers to the twilight hour, or more specifically a time so dim that it becomes difficult to distinguish people's faces.

3 These words appear in English in Nakahira's original text. He seems to be recalling the poem "Do Not Go Gentle into That Good Night" by the Welsh poet Dylan Thomas.

Index

Page references in *italics* refer to illustrations. Numbers followed by n indicate notes.

C

R

S

T

U

V

Acknowledgments

I would like to thank the people who have contributed over the past fifteen years to bringing this book into the world. This collection began in the office of Osiris in Ebisu, Tokyo, in 2009. While completing fieldwork for my PhD dissertation, I had initial conversations with Yoko Sawada about the possibility of a translation collection of Nakahira's essays. In discussions with Yoko, Akihito Yasumi, and Shino Kuraishi, whose invaluable contributions had been instrumental in expanding the understanding of Nakahira's work in Japan, we traced the contours of a Nakahira translation collection over many shared meals between 2009 and 2017. I completed some of the initial translations of Nakahira's essays for Osiris's 2010 republication of *For a Language to Come* and for the 2012 publication *Circulation: Date, Place, Events*.

Daniel Abbe, Michael K. Bourdaghs, Junnan Chen, and Phil Kaffen (including additional translations of essays not yet published by Mycah Brazelton-Braxton and Miyabi Goto) made extraordinary contributions of draft translations independently during 2016. A viable format for this collection was nurtured through conversations with Lesley A. Martin and Michael Famighetti at Aperture in New York in 2017. I am grateful for the supportive input from these two editors who recognized the vital role Nakahira played in the history of photography.

The collection came into view all the more clearly with the involvement of Daniel (who was then completing his PhD dissertation on Japanese photography) in early December of 2019, just weeks before the onset of the global COVID-19 pandemic, when we settled key aspects of the collection over a meal with Yoko in Nezu, Tokyo. Daniel then carefully edited prior translation drafts and completed the remaining translation of these essays in 2023 and 2024, making it possible to see the entire scope of Nakahira's writings for the first time. Noa Lin skillfully guided the project at Aperture, and Marc Feustel's sharp copyediting improved the texts further.

This collection materializes the collaborative work of Daniel, myself, and Yoko and is shaped by the shared dreaming at the heart of all translations. I am profoundly grateful for the generosity of Gen Nakahira that has allowed our shared dreams of this collection to become a reality. —Franz Prichard

At the Limits of the Gaze
Selected Writings by Takuma Nakahira
Edited and translated by Daniel Abbe and Franz Prichard

Front cover: Takuma Nakahira, *Untitled* (detail), from the photobook *For a Language to Come*, 1970

Editorial Adviser: Yoko Sawada
Project Editor: Noa Lin
Designer: Pacific
Typesetter: Tina Henderson, Miko McGinty Inc.
Production Consultant: Thomas Bollier
Copy Chief: Susan Ciccotti
Copy Editor: Marc Feustel
Indexer: Cathy Dorsey
Proofreaders: Hilary Becker, Freddy Martinez, Claire Voon

All essays by Takuma Nakahira translated from the Japanese by Daniel Abbe and Franz Prichard.

Additional staff of the Aperture book program includes:
Sarah Meister, Executive Director; Michael Famighetti, Editor in Chief; Sang Patten, Managing Editor, Books; Brendan Embser, Senior Editor; Karina Eckmeier, Senior Designer ; Minjee Cho, Production Director; Andrea Chlad, Production Manager; Kellie McLaughlin, Director of Sales and Outreach; Richard Gregg, Director of Book Sales and Operations

Special thanks:
The translation of the essays by Takuma Nakahira was made possible with the support of the Toshiaki Ogasawara Memorial Foundation.

This volume is part of *Aperture Ideas: Writers and Artists on Photography*, a series devoted to the finest critical and creative minds exploring key concepts in photography.

First edition, 2025
Printed in Hong Kong
10 9 8 7 6 5 4 3 2 1

Library of Congress Cataloging-in-Publication Data available upon request.

ISBN 978-1-59711-578-0

To order Aperture books, or inquire about gift or group orders, contact:
orders@aperture.org

For information about Aperture trade distribution worldwide, visit:
aperture.org/distribution

aperture

380 Columbus Avenue
New York, NY 10024
aperture.org

Aperture is a nonprofit publisher dedicated to creating insight, community, and understanding through photography.

APERTURE IDEAS

Writers and Artists on Photography

Light Matters: Writings on Photography
Essays by Vicki Goldberg

Crisis of the Real: Writings on Photography
Essays by Andy Grundberg

Between the Eyes: Essays on Photography and Politics
By David Levi Strauss
Introduction by John Berger

John Berger: Understanding a Photograph
Edited and introduced by Geoff Dyer

In Our Own Image
Essays by Fred Ritchin

Bending the Frame: Photojournalism, Documentary, and the Citizen
By Fred Ritchin

Words Not Spent Today Buy Smaller Images Tomorrow: Essays on the Present and Future of Photography
By David Levi Strauss

Photography After Frank
Essays by Philip Gefter

We Were Here: Sexuality, Photography, and Cultural Difference
Selected Writings by Sunil Gupta

Strange Hours: Photography, Memory, and the Lives of Artists
Selected Writings by Rebecca Bengal